Jeffrey D. Roth, MD

Group Psychotherapy
and Recovery from Addiction
Carrying the Message

Pre-publication
REVIEWS,
COMMENTARIES,
EVALUATIONS . . .

"Jeffrey D. Roth has written a challenging and provocative text on group psychotherapy and addiction recovery. The reader will join his group, coming right into the room to learn, by experience, just how much of addiction, recovery, and psychotherapy comes down to paradox and letting go, for both the client and the therapist.

Dr. Roth turns the reader's thinking and attention inward; one cannot get through this book without self-reflection, virtually with every page. This book is full of important lessons for every therapist."

Stephanie Brown, PhD
Director, The Addictions Institute,
Menlo Park, CA

"Dr. Roth uses an experiential device that pulls the reader into a group process that unfolds as the book progresses. He uses the responses, struggles, and experiences of group members and readers to illustrate possibilities and principles of group therapy for people with addictions.

Most books on the topic are linear in their style and delivery. This book is circular and thus challenges the reader to learn experientially as well as cognitively. *Group Psychotherapy and Recovery from Addiction* is a worthy contribution to the sparse literature on group therapy of addiction."

Charles L. Whitfield, MD
Author, *The Truth About Depression*
and *The Truth About Mental Illness*

The Haworth Press®
New York • London • Oxford

Group Psychotherapy and Recovery from Addiction
Carrying the Message

THE HAWORTH PRESS
Addiction and Group Psychotherapy
Philip Flores, PhD
Senior Editor

Group Psychotherapy and Recovery from Addiction: Carrying the Message by Jeffrey D. Roth

Other Titles of Related Interest

Group Psychotherapy with Addicted Populations: An Integration of Twelve-Step and Psychodynamic Theory, Second Edition by Philip J. Flores

Treating Co-Occurring Disorders: A Handbook for Mental Health and Substance Abuse Professionals by Edward L. Hendrickson, Marilyn S. Schmal, and Sharon C. Ekleberry

The Group Therapy of Substance Abuse edited by David W. Brook and Henry I. Spitz

Managing the Dually Diagnosed Patient: Current Issues and Clinical Approaches, Second Edition edited by David F. O'Connell and Eileen P. Beyer

Solution-Focused Brief Therapy: Its Effective Use in Agency Settings by Teri Pichot and Yvonne M. Dolan

Alcoholism, Drug Addiction, and the Road to Recovery: Life on the Edge by Barry Stimmel

Group Psychotherapy and Recovery from Addiction
Carrying the Message

Jeffrey D. Roth, MD

Routledge
Taylor & Francis Group

LONDON AND NEW YORK

First published 2004
by The Haworth Press, Inc.

Published 2016 by Routledge
2 Park Square, Milton Park, Abingdon, Oxon OX14 4RN
711 Third Avenue, New York, NY, 10017, USA

Routledge is an imprint of the Taylor & Francis Group, an informa business

The Twelve Steps and Twelve Traditions are reprinted with permission of Alcoholics Anonymous World Services, Inc. (AAWS). Permission to reprint the Twelve Steps and Twelve Traditions does not mean that AAWS has reviewed or approved the contents of this publication, or that AA necessarily agrees with the views expressed herein. AA is a program of recovery from alcoholism *only*—use of the Twelve Steps and Twelve Traditions in connection with programs and activities which are patterned after AA, but which address other problems, or in any other non-AA context, does not imply otherwise.

Al-Anon meeting format reprinted by permission of Al-Anon Family Group Headquarters, Inc.

PUBLISHER'S NOTE
The members of the group in this book reside solely in this book. Any resemblance to yourself or anyone you know is entirely a consequence of our being more alike as human beings than we are different.

Cover design by Marylouise E. Doyle.

Library of Congress Cataloging-in-Publication Data

Roth, Jeffrey D., 1953-
    Group psychotherapy and recovery from addiction : carrying the message / Jeffrey D. Roth.
        p. ; cm.
Includes bibliographical references and index.
    1. Substance abuse—Treatment. 2. Group psychotherapy. 3. Twelve-step programs.
        [DNLM: 1. Alcoholics Anonymous. 2. Substance-Related Disorders—therapy. 3. Psychotherapy, Group. 4. Self-Help Groups. 5. Substance-Related Disorders—psychology. WM 270 R8455g 2004] I. Title.
RC564.R686 2004
616.86'0651—dc21

                                                                                2003012240

ISBN 13: 978-0-789-01644-7 (hbk)
ISBN 13: 978-0-789-01645-4 (pbk)

To Tamara, my wife and partner
in giving birth to this book

ABOUT THE AUTHOR

Jeffrey D. Roth, MD, is an addictions psychiatrist and group psychotherapist. He graduated from Yale University Medical School and did his residency in psychiatry at the University of Chicago. Dr. Roth is board certified in psychiatry and in the sub-specialty of addictions psychiatry, and is certified and recertified in addictions medicine by the American Society of Addictions Medicine (ASAM). He is the chairperson of the Family and Generational Issues Committee of ASAM and a Fellow of the American Group Psychotherapy Association.

CONTENTS

Foreword

Early in this book, the author states that addiction is fundamentally a disease of isolation. With this statement, Jeffrey Roth quickly moves to the core of this book and why group psychotherapy is such an effective modality for the treatment of addiction. Historically, group treatment and addiction have always shared a long and complementary relationship. Ever since addiction first came to be recognized as a diagnostic entity, its treatment has been conducted primarily in groups. Consequently, unlike other diagnostic categories, group therapy has never had to fight to prove its legitimacy as a viable treatment option. Like magnets, group therapy and addiction treatment have always been drawn to each other because the inherent qualities of group treatment lend themselves in a synergistic and complementary way to the innate dynamics that drive the addiction process. Dr. Roth's book helps us understand why this is so.

The concept that addiction is both a solution to and a consequence of an impaired ability to establish and maintain relationships is implied throughout Dr. Roth's book. Accordingly, he builds a convincing case through his clinical illustrations that if abstinence and recovery are to be achieved and maintained, the addicted individual must develop the capacity to establish healthy, emotionally regulatory relationships. Group therapy, as Dr. Roth clearly demonstrates, is the ideal vehicle for accomplishing this end.

As Roth implies with his declaration that "individuals do not recover; groups recover," addiction treatment cannot be successfully accomplished unless a commitment is made by the addicted individual to be in a relationship with a person rather than a drug of choice. As long as addicted individuals remain attached to their drugs, they will not be able to attach to anyone else or to a culture of recovery. As Alcoholics Anonymous has maintained for decades, the alcoholic must first *detach* from the object of addiction before a therapeutic alliance can be formed. Without an alliance, any hope of treatment is impossible. Again, Dr. Roth captures this principle when he deftly

writes that addiction is a " . . . disease that was designed to interfere
with attachment." When the addict or alcoholic even considers attaching to something other than the drug of choice, this in itself is
a powerful step in the direction of recovery. Groups composed of
individuals struggling with similar difficulties with detachment and
attachment are better able to accomplish this task because groups
reduce the sense of isolation and shame that accompanies every addictive process.

This book, however, is far more than just another text about addiction. It is about the power inherent in a group—whether that group be
a therapy group, a family, a community, or society at large—to provide an essential ingredient in what it means to be a healthy, fully
functioning adult. In a highly original and creative style, Jeffrey Roth
invites and allows us to be part of a group in "real time" as we engage
him and the other group members in a dialogue that comes alive on
the pages before us.

If the reader is looking for a text that offers easy, perfect solutions
for either addiction or its treatment, this is not the book for you. Dr.
Roth's approach to the subject is neither simplistic or reductionistic.
Dr. Roth clearly understands the many complexities of addictive behavior and how these complexities interact with the dynamics of individual personality development and the dynamics inherently evoked
in any group situation. Dr. Roth explores, compares, and dissects
these multiple contrasting and sometimes clashing circumstances as
they arise in the group setting. His unflinching examinations of the
interactions that an open and authentic group culture can generate
constantly remind the reader that behind every addict and alcoholic is
a suffering individual who is striving to break out of isolation and
connect to someone and something larger than the self. Paradoxi-
cally, by breaking through the isolation of one's addiction, group
members eventually develop a more authentic relationship with themselves.

Roth's rich and colorful clinical examples reveal the often difficult,
but authentic exchanges between his group members, and Roth, the
group leader, has obviously created an ideal group environment that
allows group members to freely speak their minds. The open and
honest exchanges that occur in Roth's group do not happen by
chance. They result from and are reflective of a group leader's skill in

establishing the proper therapeutic group culture, one that permits its members to openly challenge one another and the group leader in a direct, authentic manner, but without malice or intent to hurt. It is obvious that Roth has guided the group and its members to establish the kind of intimacy and emotional honesty that is too often missing in most people's lives, whether they are addicted or not.

Dr. Roth often challenges conventional wisdom about addiction and requires active participation by those who can respond to his innovative and thought-provoking style. As I suggested earlier, those readers looking for a text that offers effortless "how-to" answers to addiction treatment will be disappointed. Rather, Jeffrey Roth challenges the reader to join him in a collaborative effort that may at first baffle and confuse the less adventurous. I urge readers to leave the written world of certainty and follow this pied piper into the chaotic world of uncertainty that accompanies all authentic encounters and relationships. The rewards will be enormous.

Philip J. Flores, PhD, ABPP, CGP, FAGPA

Preface

Most of the ideas I describe in this book I have presented to professional and nonprofessional groups before. I usually invite my audience to ask any questions that arise about my presentation immediately. I do this because my experience is that each idea is part of a sequence that builds a foundation for the next idea. So I prefer to have an argument about a fundamental concept early in the presentation, rather than have a misunderstanding arise at the end of our work together, which topples our fragile alliance like a house of cards.

While I admit my powerlessness over how this book is read, my preference is that you pay close attention to any statement or concept read here that does not "sit well." You may choose to bypass such discomfort by adopting a willing suspension of disbelief, only to find that you must reject everything I offer here when your disbelief is resumed at the end of the book. As long as I am suggesting how not to read this book, I also humbly ask that you consider reading this book with at least one other person. Then, when questions arise, you can turn to your fellow reader(s) and begin an experiential examination of your discomfort.

Fellow readers may be found in your own social network. I have also set up space on the bulletin board page of the Web site <www.workingsobriety.com>. There you will be able to read and post questions and comments, and communicate with other readers in a virtual group in cyberspace via e-mail or the Web site chat room.

A word of caution: this book is not intended to be a self-help book. I am offering a means of accessing greater depth of appreciation for the richness of group life, specifically via group psychotherapy and Twelve-Step recovery. No book could substitute for these face-to-face, spontaneous, intimate experiences.

A Note About the Fonts

I use Times Roman when I am writing to you, the reader.

Times Roman italicized indicates that I am speaking to you and the other members of the group.

My name is Kelly and my font is Comic Sans MS, probably because Dr. Roth is making fun of me.

I'm Richard and my font, Monotype Corsiva, bears a suspicious resemblance to Times Roman italicized. Maybe Roth is indicating how identified we are with each other.

Hi. Bea is my name and Mistral is my game. Underneath my taking care of you I can stir up a storm.

Warren here. Haettenschweiler is my voice. Dark, husky, aggressive.

I'm Leslie. I speak in Arial Narrow. Sort of halfway between Kelly and Warren.

I'm Chris, just visiting. My font is Greymantle; just think of me as coming from some grey territory outside of this book.

When all of us speak in one voice, you will experience many different flavors. That's why our font is Spumoni.

And you, the reader, get to express yourself in what else, Bookman Old Style.

Acknowledgments

My first thanks go to Philip Flores, editor, and The Haworth Press, publisher, for supporting me in creating this book from its inception.

It takes a village to raise an author. From the village of New Haven, Connecticut, I thank Boris Astrachan, Marshall Edelson, and Bernard Snow for providing a foundation in group process and an understanding of social systems. From the village of Chicago, Illinois, I offer credit to the late Samuel Lipton and to the very present Leo Sadow for whatever wisdom I have garnered about psychoanalysis. The same credit belongs to Robert Lipgar, my steadfast supervisor, mentor, and guide in the territory between group psychotherapy and group relations conference work. To these intellectual parents I express gratitude for their contributions to this book. For its flaws I remain solely responsible.

These flaws persist in spite of the commitment of the group that supports me in the writing. This loyal group of colleagues, led by Jerome Beigler, includes Joe Check, Ned Ellefson, Christine Kieffer, Norman Kohn, Kevin Murphy, and Jim Tifft. They form the first group of readers and their comments have given a shape to the book which I hope renders it more welcoming to readers.

Finally, my undying love to countless anonymous contributors whose stories and feelings provide the backbone to whatever message of recovery I have been able to carry in this book.

The Twelve Steps and the Twelve Traditions are reprinted with permission of Alcoholics Anonymous World Services, Inc. (AAWS). Permission to reprint the Twelve Steps and the Twelve Traditions does not mean that AAWS has reviewed or approved the contents of this publication, or that AA necessarily agrees with the views expressed herein. AA is a program of recovery from alcoholism *only*— use of the Twelve Steps and Twelve Traditions in connection with programs and activities which are patterned after AA, but which address other problems, or in any other non-AA context, does not imply otherwise.

Chapter 1

Addiction As a Family Disease

Did you read the preface? If not, please return to the preface before proceeding with this chapter. I make this request to raise awareness that in reading this book you are joining a group. You may choose to believe that you are reading this book alone, privately, in isolation. Alternatively, even if you are the only reader, I suggest that you and I have formed a group consisting of author and reader. Inevitably, you and I have been members of many different groups: our original families, social groups, work and professional groups, therapy groups, self-help groups, and other groups in which our membership may have occurred without intention or awareness. Because this book is first and foremost an investigation of group functioning, I want to make explicit that this group of author and readership is occurring with both intention and awareness.

If you accept that in reading this book you are joining a group, we have made a promising beginning in our investigation of group function. Specifically, we can now examine what factors facilitate healthy group function and what factors impair group function. I invite you to work with me in making explicit what is happening right now in this newly formed relationship.

Perhaps you have been thinking that my style in writing this book is unlike your usual texts. For my part I have been wondering if I can trust you to work with me in this difficult task. Take a moment to reflect on your doubts and reservations about joining. Instead of suppressing these thoughts, say them out loud so that you can appreciate their force and vitality.

In my experience, the process of joining a group is inevitably accompanied by ambivalence, and this ambivalence is located in the group even if only an individual or a subgroup within the group overtly expresses the ambivalence. I express my ambivalence about joining this group with you by withholding unconditional trust in your willingness and ability to work with me. By withholding trust I protect myself from feeling hurt and lonely in relation to my anticipation of rejection. Perhaps you protect yourself in similar fashion, perhaps differently.

If you are not aware of any ambivalence whatsoever about joining me, then you may trust that I am carrying ambivalence for both of us. Alternatively, you might conclude that you are simply a completely sane and rational individual confronted with a crazy author. In this latter case, we have now located your ambivalence about joining me in the notion that I am crazy.

The concept of an individual or subgroup carrying something on behalf of a group is central to group psychotherapy and Twelve-Step recovery. We will look at how a group carries the message of recovery in Chapter 2. First let us turn our attention to how our group carries the message of dis-ease (henceforth expressed in its more usual spelling, disease).

Two models prevail in our everyday explanations of human behavior, and these models are then applied to our understanding of disease and addiction. The first model asserts that our behavior is governed internally by free will; each individual operates autonomously and voluntarily. This moral model assumes many forms in different systems, including religious and humanistic. The second model asserts that our behavior is governed by some source that is external to our selves; each individual's behavior is determined by some formula as yet unknown. This deterministic model likewise assumes many forms, including in some places that we might not expect. We might associate determinism only with a religious philosophy that posits a white-bearded controller of our destinies. However, in our current romance with molecular genetics, some of us unwittingly adopt a biological determinism in which DNA governs our behavior. Ironically, both the moral model and the deterministic models share a common feature. Disease in general and addiction in particular become manifestations of badness in the individual, either badness of conduct or badness of genes.

Neither of these models of human behavior accounts for the complexity of social systems. Let us return to our relationship in our group. Are you forcing yourself to read these words? Did you come to this book by yourself or were you influenced by your experiences in groups, your professional training, your recovery, or other social factors to enter this group with me? Is reading this particular book inscribed in your DNA? For me, writing this book seems to be a product of all of my experiences in groups. I was not ready to write five years ago. Did my DNA change in that time? I suspect that I am writing now as a way to attach to you, which I do with my own limitations, imperfections, and disease.

My attachment to you offers me a third alternative model to explain my behavior. Perhaps I am not writing this book by force of will, alone and independently. Perhaps I have a relationship with my editor and my publisher. I might share my writing with colleagues, friends, and family. These attachments might authorize and empower me to engage with you right now. You may likewise have been influenced to read this book by a direct or indirect relationship with the editor, the publisher, colleagues, friends, family, and me. What I emphasize here is the possibility that neither of us joined our group by ourselves, in isolation. You need me in order to read this book with me. I need you in order to write this book with you.

What other kinds of disease might interfere or disrupt our work together? If you authorize me to offer you some useful experience about groups, you might want my attention focused on our task. If I am at this moment drinking alcohol, using drugs, eating compulsively, preoccupied with sex, money, work, or my impaired family member, I might not be fully available to engage with or attach to you. If you become preoccupied with the idea that I am distracted in any of these ways, your preoccupation might disrupt your ability to engage with or attach to me. If we keep the focus on us as a group, rather than on either of us as individuals, then whatever is interfering with my ability to work with you may generate disease in our group, and the extent to which you become preoccupied with this interference may also be symptomatic of this same disease process.

I propose a thought experiment. Imagine: *I am now polishing off a fifth of Scotch. My editor has been kind enough to correct my numerous typographical and grammatical errors; you cannot smell the alcohol on my breath through these pages, and you cannot see the glassy look in my eyes. I have succeeded in overcoming my overwhelming terror of writing this book, but I am paying for my intoxica-*

tion with an irritatingly garrulous style. Are you reminding yourself
that this is only a thought experiment? Are you wondering whether
this mad author is desperately confessing his uncontrolled drinking?

If you can imagine yourself engaged in these thought processes,
you may be able to appreciate the impact of alcohol entering into our
group. If we extend this thought experiment, but now you are the one
polishing off the fifth of Scotch, we might adopt a more inclusive attitude toward the presence of this third member of our small group, the
fifth of Scotch. I suggest that to the extent that this fifth of Scotch im-
pairs our work together, which one of us is doing the drinking is irrelevant. We may both suffer from the presence of this third member,
this fifth of Scotch, this symbol of disease. We have encountered a
group disease. If our group were a family, we would be suffering from
a family disease.

You may object now, claiming that the question of who is drinking
is of paramount importance. After all, you point out, only one of us
will wake up tomorrow with a violent hangover. I respond (gently, I
trust) that you are mistaken on two counts. First, that for the purposes
of this particular moment, having a hangover tomorrow is irrelevant. I
am only concerned with how we are functioning as a group right now.
Second, even if I reluctantly allow you to drag me kicking and
screaming into the future, both of us will suffer tomorrow from contact with our mutual friend alcohol today. If I have the hangover, you
may need to question whether your time and energy has been well invested in reading about group function or intoxication. If you have
the hangover, I may need to question whether my time and energy has
been well invested in writing to someone in a blackout who may not
even remember ever having picked up this book.

Let us pause here. I teased you just now about dragging me kicking
and screaming into the future. Sometimes the process of joining a
group may be experienced as dragging oneself or dragging someone
else into a process kicking and screaming. I hope I have clearly stated
my premise that this process of joining and attaching to a group is
central to an understanding of addiction, recovery, and group psychotherapy. As a physician, I believe in informed consent. Therefore, as
an author, I believe you deserve to know where I see us going together
if you accept the premise that we are now in a group together. On the
horizon I see us finding that:

1. Addiction is fundamentally a disease of isolation.
2. Isolation is defined in terms of the individual's relationship to the group.
3. Isolation of any group member or subgroup reflects an impairment in the group's ability to include that member or subgroup.

If we accept these first three premises, we may also find that:

4. Addiction is a disease of the group.
5. Individuals do not recover; groups recover.

Now that I have put my cards on the table, you may have two reactions. The first reaction might be, what was all this fuss about? Nothing is controversial here yet. Okay, I am part of the group and let us get on with the matter at hand. The second reaction might be, do not tell me I cannot recover without a group. I may need others for some aspects of my life, but in other aspects I am doing very well by myself, thank you.

If you are not able to see yourself at this point as part of a group, I strongly recommend that you reconsider your decision to read this book alone. On the other hand, if you cannot identify with the wish to withhold a part of yourself from this project, you are the first perfect human being I have the honor to encounter. In case you are this perfect human being, and because we have paused for a moment anyway, I will share a story with you.

I was going to see a patient for the first time in consultation. The door to my waiting room from the outside hallway was made of translucent glass. When I opened the door from my consultation room to the waiting room, I saw that the waiting room was empty. I noticed, however, through the translucent door to the hallway, that someone was standing right outside the door. I invited the woman in, ascertaining that she was the patient whom I was going to see. Following this consultation appointment, I accepted her as a patient. After more than a year of treatment, I noticed that while she seemed to be able to associate freely (see Chapter 3), she did not respond to my interpretations and I realized that I was confused about why she was a patient. I decided to ask her why she was seeing me, and she replied, "I did not want to see you. The only reason I am here is because you invited me in."

Unless you are also reading this book only by invitation, we may continue now with our examination of addiction as a family disease. I

offer you what I consider to be some indices of healthy group function, contrasted with some corresponding indices of diseased group
function:

1. *A healthy group operates for the benefit of all of its members.*
Members are able to assume roles that fit their abilities, and all members receive support from the group to perform their tasks. Consider
the group that resides in each cell of our body. This group includes a
nucleus, ribosomes, mitochondria, a cell membrane, and other cell
constituents. Each member of this group has a role suited to its structure and composition. No member is superfluous; all members need
one another's participation to maintain adequate healthy cellular
(group) function.

The group becomes diseased when any member is unable to carry
out its role in supporting the group effectively. Suppose that the cell is
in a body that is smoking a cigarette. The cell is exposed to nicotine, a
metabolic poison, which interferes with the mitochondrion's role of
transforming fuel into energy. The other members of the cellular
group gradually adapt to the presence of its nicotine-impaired mitochondria by making demands for more fuel, and the body that is smoking cigarettes finds itself burning its stored fat (losing weight) or increasing its food intake.

As long as we are considering the impact of nicotine on the cellular
group, we may as well look at its impact on groups of humans. Two
groups of humans in particular have suffered from the impact of nicotine's psychopharmacological effect on interpersonal chemistry. Ironically, these two groups are mental health professionals and substance
abuse treatment providers, as well as many of the clients that both
groups treat. Nicotine is an emotional poison, which interferes with
the individual's ability to transform experience into emotion. An il-
lustration of this mode of action of nicotine is available in the group
consisting of condemned prisoner and firing squad. The prisoner is
offered a cigarette prior to execution to short-circuit his terror. The
firing squad can then kill the prisoner without risk of identifying with
him, because the emotional glue that holds the group together as a
family of human beings has been dissolved.

Continuing with the theme of addiction as a family disease, the
disruption by nicotine of intimacy in the therapeutic relationship is
equally effective whether the therapist or client is under the influence

of nicotine. I suspect that the use of nicotine has protected generations of therapists and clients from the intimacy that arises effortlessly in the therapeutic encounter. Thus, whether I am smoking while writing this book or you are smoking while reading it, in either case we are both enveloped in a cloud of smoke that will interfere with a clear examination of our feelings, and therefore interfere with our attachment.

   2. *A healthy group has the capacity to regulate its boundaries effectively.*

   I wrote this last sentence about an hour before two hijacked airliners crashed into the World Trade Center. I am now leaving my downtown Chicago office early respecting my powerlessness over my nation's inability to regulate its boundaries, and respecting the love of family and friends who wanted me away from tall buildings. I have called each of my patients to cancel our appointments for today; making contact with them as best I can reflects my commitment to these relationships, as leaving downtown Chicago now reflects my commitment to relationships with family and friends. How then do I respect the commitment I have made to you, the commitment to write to you and share the process of joining this group with you?

   Join me then, in what is now my present time, what will be the near or distant past for you: Tuesday, September 11, 2001. I suspect that wherever you are today, at this moment, that you are like me, in shock. People around us share the widest range of feelings. Many of us feel terror. Some react to the terror by shutting down, becoming numb. Others are becoming hypervigilant. A few people are feeling sadness, crying. Some are enraged or outraged. As in the case of many crises, most of us are a little more sensitive to other people, and we reach out cautiously, not wanting to be isolated ourselves in the intensity of our feelings.

   Then, still in shock, or emerging from shock, we look for some meaning, some way to make sense of the chaos and overwhelming emotions. As I write this description to you, I am aware that one way for me to cope with the assault on our national boundaries is to focus on the task at hand, my one small piece of reality that would otherwise be totally consumed by this catastrophe. The challenge at this moment is the same challenge that any group faces, whether experiencing calm or crisis.

How do we regulate the boundaries of our group so that these boundaries remain semipermeable? A semipermeable boundary retains within the group and brings into the group the components and support that the group needs for survival. The semipermeable boundary also protects the group from harmful or toxic effects, and eliminates toxic products from the group. With an impermeable boundary the group starves for nourishment and suffocates in its own waste.

At least two aspects of our nation's boundary regulation are relevant here. First, an enormous amount of energy has been invested in preventing airline hijacking, not to speak of preventing the use of such airplanes to perpetrate wholesale slaughter and destruction. Yet we have maintained, and we will likely continue to maintain, boundaries that are permeable enough to allow the unthinkable to occur. Second, and perhaps more significantly, we expend much of our emotional energy directed toward defending ourselves from attack from the outside, leaving ourselves vulnerable to the more probable attack from within us. I suggest that multiple layers of collusion on our part exist as necessary ingredients to this tragedy. I suggest this not in the spirit of blaming ourselves, but in the service of maintaining semipermeable boundaries. I watch today as most of my immediate environment is shutting down. Flags are flying half-mast. In tandem with needing to pause, rest, and recover from the shock, we must also maintain hope that our connection can persist intact.

3. *Hope for the future is an experience that we might associate with generativity and reproduction, which provide a third index of healthy group function.* A healthy group has the capacity to import new members across semipermeable boundaries. These new members are assimilated into the group. As the group enlarges, it prepares for reproduction by generating a differentiated membership that can fill all of the necessary roles for two separate groups to function.

Returning to the cellular metaphor, when the cell is reproducing during mitosis, each component of the cell must be replicated so that each offspring has a nucleus, ribosomes, mitochondria, cell membrane, and the rest of the complement of cellular constituents. Ideally this succession occurs collaboratively, each cellular constituent supporting the process of reproduction. Similarly, in a well-functioning group, members support one another in developing the necessary skills to provide leadership, direction, boundary regulation, and re-productive capacity for the offspring of that group.

Sterility is one symptom of diseased group function. The group ex-presses its ambivalence about joining together by failing to cooperate and support each member in accomplishing the tasks necessary for group function. Boundaries may be vague and porous to the point of leaving the group poorly defined, or so rigid that the group is unable to import new members to support succession. Note that group repro-duction does not necessarily entail creation of two separate groups. Sometimes reproduction may simply look like replacing a group member with another member. This substitution alters the original group, and we may consider this altered group the offspring of the first one.

I offer you now two examples of diseased group function from my own experience. Both groups are professional groups. Group A is part of a national medical organization that put together group A to advise the organization on matters relating to family violence. Group B is a regional group belonging to a national organization whose task is the examination of group process. Each group exhibits dysfunction in each of the three indices described above: mutual support or inter-dependence, boundary regulation, and generativity.

Group A formed in response to heightened national awareness about domestic or family violence. Key members of this national or-ganization had some personal experience with family violence, while other members professed a more academic or research interest in the area. The national medical organization, which is composed of a con-federation of state medical societies and specialty societies, asked these groups to send representatives to group A, which became a group of about thirty members meeting twice a year. Group A spends about 90 percent of its time and energy together on two issues, resolv-ing neither. First the representatives give reports about the activity of their own state or specialty society that relates to family violence. No unifying connection is created or even apparently desired. The group seemingly gets together in order not to join. Significantly, no evi-dence of conflict emerges, and the group actively avoids any sugges-tion of conflict. I speculate that the group needs to suppress conflict to avoid the fantasized consequence of violence that is the experience for those group members who have had personal experience of violence associated with conflict.

Not surprisingly, the group also has great difficulty managing its boundaries. When it is not preoccupied with presentation of disconnected individual activities, the group engages in endless proposals for inviting some other organization to join the group. Whether the group wants to invite a representative from the legal profession, the clergy, or a grassroots organization, the group seems incapable of examining its difficulty using its existing membership to address the task of advising the national organization. The subjects that seem to be taboo for this group are any personal experience of family violence, any feelings about this personal experience, or any examination of the manner in which these experiences might be being reenacted (see Chapter 7) by the group.

Group B exhibits difficulties that are the opposite of Group A. About twenty members who were all students of the group's two leaders, Dr. Clark and Dr. Drake, formed group B. The group had a national counterpart, but did not affiliate or join for a couple of years. The ambivalence about joining the national organization was mirrored by the uneasy alliance between Drs. Clark and Drake, and the inability of the students of these leaders to join one group for their common welfare. The major task of the group had been to organize group relations conferences, yet Drs. Clark and Drake would consistently perform this task apart from group B. With few exceptions, Dr. Clark or Dr. Drake would also direct conferences. The other members of group B act as if no other means of organizing or directing a conference is available to them, despite alternative models existing in other parts of the national organization. The apparent total dependence on Drs. Clark and Drake belies a near complete inability of the group members to work interdependently.

The boundary regulation of group B also suffers from its dependence on Drs. Clark and Drake. While in principle anyone with the requisite experience in group relations conference work may join group B, in practice entry into the group occurs through being a student of these leaders, or by being a student of one of their students. One member who entered the group from another city, where he had belonged to an analogous group, became the target of vicious scapegoating. Not surprisingly, he was quite critical of the group leaders, and he was unable to see the complicity of the group in using him to voice the group's unmanageability in its relationship with its leaders.

These three indices of group function and group disease have been described in the group analytic literature as aspects of the group's basic assumptions. As originally developed by Wilfred Bion (1961) and detailed in his book *Experience in Groups,* basic assumptions are covert group processes that coexist with the manifest work function of the group. The basic assumptions are dependence, fight-flight, and pairing.

In basic assumption dependence, the group acts as if its primary task were to find someone or something on which the group could depend to take care of all of its needs. In a healthy group, basic assumption dependence is explicit insofar as each member of the group can depend on all other members and on the group as a whole to provide support in working toward the group's primary task. In the diseased group, basic assumption dependence is implicit in the group's functioning. For example, in group A described previously, the group acts as if some delegate of another outside organization would solve the group's problems. In group B, members act as if the sole source of support emanates from Drs. Clark and Drake.

Note that the impairment in boundary regulation for each of these groups mirrors the form of its maladaptive dependence. In group A, well-defined boundaries cannot be established because of the belief that salvation depends upon some as yet unrecognized savior who is still outside the group. In group B, conflict between the two saviors (Drs. Clark and Drake) demands rigid boundaries because of the belief that the survival of the group depends on keeping its saviors locked in the group in mortal combat.

When the group is engaged in basic assumption fight-flight, it acts as if it had an enemy that it had to engage in combat or escape from. Survival of the group is therefore assumed to hinge on dealing with the enemy rather than engaging in the work task of the group. This enemy must be defeated or avoided at all costs.

The healthy group maintains a balanced awareness of basic assumption fight-flight. Effective boundary regulation relies critically on the group's ability to join together in the service of a mutually negotiated task. The group's task determines what the group needs in order to work and what will interfere with the group's work. For the task in our group in this book of examining and understanding group process and recovery from addiction, we need for me to write and for you to read. We have also considered the possibility that a fifth of Scotch would interfere with our work. If we are regulating our group boundaries effectively, these boundaries will be constructed in order to support our continuing presence and activity in this group, and to effortlessly let go of the fifth of Scotch. Effective boundary regulation relies critically on the group's ability to refuse admittance, or avoid, toxic substances and to eject from the group elements that interfere with the group's work.

In the diseased group, the priority of fighting with the enemy overrides all other aspects of adaptive group function. Note the paradox that fighting with the enemy leads inevitably to making the enemy into an honored member of the group. In group A, the interminable recitation of individual members' organizational activities is an expression of basic assumption fight-flight. The group uses these recitations to run away from its task of joining to examine family violence and scatters its energy on unrelated missions. In group B, the use of a scapegoated member as an enemy organizes the group in a fight with the scapegoat, and also covertly with Drs. Clark and Drake whom the group attacks using the scapegoat as a hit man. Note also that basic assumption dependence is characteristically a passive resistance to work in the diseased group, while the healthy group actively uses dependence in the service of group work. Similarly, basic assumption fight-flight is generally an active resistance to work in the diseased group, with substantial effort expended in combat with or avoidance of the enemy. On the other hand, the healthy group is virtually passive in its use of fight-flight, because the healthy group has boundaries that effortlessly exclude toxicity and maintain an internal environment that does not favor the accumulation of disruptive waste.

Two examples of how a group manages internally disruptive processes may be useful. The group that consists of the organ systems of the human body has delegated much of the function of waste management to one of its members, the liver. This member uses its talents to filter toxins out of its fellow group member, the circulatory system, whose blood carries numerous components that are toxic to the whole group. The body does not condemn the blood for carrying poison because the body has delegated to the blood the role of transporting both nourishment and poison from one member of the body to other members. The liver welcomes the blood, extracts the poison, and metabolizes the poison into a form that can be either used or excreted.

Likewise, a group may handle conflict and its by-products collaboratively or dysfunctionally. A healthy group engages in conflict with an appreciation that the conflict affects the group as a whole. No individual member receives blame or condemnation. The group supports the function of members in different roles, with some members carrying the conflict and others metabolizing the conflict so that the whole group is able to resolve the conflict. I suggest that on a group level what we mean by conflict resolution is the extraction from a conflict of precisely that part of the conflict that nurtures group function, and the metabolism of the toxic part so that the toxicity can be excreted from the group. The mechanism for metabolizing and excreting toxicities will be described in more detail in Chapter 7 as reenactment.

Pairing defines the simplest unit of joining. This act of two individuals uniting for a common purpose is the necessary and sufficient condition for reproduction to occur. Short of recourse to parthenogenesis, we may agree that pairing is necessary for reproduction. You might, however, insist that pairing is not sufficient for the production of offspring. I remind you at this point that you and I have become a pair, the smallest group, and that our offspring is that group itself which takes material form in this book. Our pairing cannot occur without both of us surrendering to basic assumption dependence and fight-flight. For the work of this book to proceed, I need to depend on your reading it and you need to depend on my writing it. Our dependence, by the way, is not merely dependence on the mechanical acts of reading and writing. We need each other to be fully present. You do not want me launching off on some idiosyncratic tangent without you. I want more than the residual attention you might be able to give me if you were reading this book while watching a baseball game at the stadium with 100,000 screaming fans. Therefore, we are both constructing a boundary around our group work together that protects us from being distracted from our task, and enables us to deal with elements of our relationship that impede our task.

Ironically, in basic assumption pairing, the group acts as if the group could be miraculously rescued from stagnancy by the pairing of two members who would produce a messianic offspring. The group then elects a couple to engage in pairing, with the rest of the group participating vicariously, passively, and voyeuristically in the ritual mating. I hope that you are seeing that the problem here is not that two members are pairing, but that the rest of the group is passive. In a healthy group, all members are pairing with each other and with the group. The alternative to pairing is isolating, which leads inexorably to the death of the individual and therefore to the death of the group.

The recognition of pairing as essential to the life of the family is necessary for an appreciation of addiction as a family disease. If we focus our attention only on the activity of a dysfunctional group or family, we are likely to see the addict engaged in frantic activity, attempting to balance the demands of addiction and family role at the same time. This process often transforms the addict from a human being to a human doing. Other group or family members may also be quite busy, especially when they are balancing the demands of their own roles and picking up pieces of incomplete work (or feelings) for the addict. These members, because they are able to perform their tasks adequately, are seldom seen as having a problem, even though they are also reduced to the status of a human doing.

The behavior of group A provides an excellent example of frantic activity used to disguise an underlying fragmentation. I would add that all of the members of this group are highly socially competent people. Pairing of members among subgroups was commonplace, but these pairings never produced any experience of joining in the group as a whole. On many occasions I pointed out the futility of understanding violence as a process in family groups when we were unable to examine our own process. Each time I offered these comments, a different member of the group would approach me privately to reassure me that I was not alone in my perceptions. I understood these pairings with me as part of the group dysfunction designed to alleviate my loneliness but leave the group in isolation.

Group B adopts a different strategy in its use of pairing. The only legitimate pairing (that is, a pairing that might lead to work on the group task) seems to occur between Drs. Clark and Drake, and this pairing is unstable at best. As in group A, individuals in group B are competent and social enough to maintain relationships with each other in various informal pairings, but these pairings have never resulted in work on the group's task.

I have told you two stories about groups that I know, and I have shared a clinical story. At this point I would like to begin introducing some new members into our group. As with any group, these members may join and then leave precipitously, or they may remain with us throughout our journey together. They may be active participants or silent observers. They speak in their own voices in first person.

My name is Kelly. I have been suicidal as long as I can remember. My father killed himself with an overdose of barbiturates when I was a young adult. I have attempted suicide dozens of times, usually while I was drunk and always by taking pills. Before I stopped drinking, these suicide attempts always landed me in the hospital on the psychiatry ward where I would be diagnosed as depressed. I was seeing psychiatrists for forty years while I was drinking. They would prescribe antidepressants and sedatives.

I got married in college. My husband and I had two children soon after I graduated while my husband finished his doctorate. He became a successful professor at a prestigious university while I worked in a technical career. From time to time each of my psychiatrists would see my husband and me together, usually at my husband's insistence. He would explain to my psychiatrists how burdensome I was. He would offer examples of his suffering with the best of intentions, without rancor or malice, in order to persuade my psychiatrists that they had to help me.

I take this opportunity to alert you, in case you have been seduced into becoming interested in Kelly's story, that she has not engaged with you to join this group. Similar to the patient who needed an invitation, Kelly shares her story with you as if she were a guest. Unlike that patient, Kelly is in this group with us. I could confront her uselessly until I was blue in the face that she is not relating to us. However, because we are in a group, I have the opportunity to use Kelly's isolation creatively. I begin to use her isolation by pairing with you, who are also being ignored and isolated by Kelly. I imagine that you, like me, could be misled by Kelly's honesty about her past life in order to ignore her lack of honesty about the process of being here. As we attach regarding our sharing the task of examining our group process, and as we acknowledge our powerlessness over who joins and at what rate, we may even become able to include Kelly in our group in a meaningful way. Just as either of us may have become attached to a reporting of history devoid of genuine intimacy, so Kelly may have become attached to a series of emotionally sterile relationships: with her suicidal father, her distant psychiatrists, and her condescending husband. Apparently, we needed Kelly to join us at this point to teach us about pairing and dependence. If Kelly is able to need us the way we need her, she may succeed in joining the group.

This is a bit strange. I know that we have talked about your using me in a book, but I never imagined you would suggest me joining a book group in addition to the live one you stuck me in. I suppose it is comforting to see Kelly's familiar face, but who is this reader character that you have invited here?

Richard, don't be rude. You are going to scare our new member away.

Let go, Kelly. If Roth is going to put me in another damn group, he cannot expect me to change my personality to please some reader. Besides, you are the one who ran away from our last group.

I am grateful to hear that the group is expressing some of its anger and ambivalence about joining. I suspect, though, that blaming our silent reader for the way that I have constructed this group, and protecting the reader from feelings are both ways for the group to avoid dealing directly with me.

I confess, though, to being curious about Kelly's assumption that you would react defensively to Richard's directness. Kelly has taught me that while telling one's story may be useful in recovery, it may sometimes be used as a defense against participating in a relationship in the here and now. I have also learned that I can trust that the process of becoming intimate will progress in its own time if I can attend to what is happening at this moment. The common wisdom in Twelve-

Step programs for how to tell one's story includes three parts: my life
before recovery, how I entered recovery, and what my life is like now.
A story that dwells on the experience of addiction is called a drunk-
alog, and although this story may be entertaining or intoxicating, it
may also fail to establish a more intimate connection in the here and
now.

Chapter 2

How the Group
Carries the Message of Recovery

Congratulations! Since you have remained in this group to this point, I assume that we are now functioning as a group. Note that I have not given up my individual identity to be a member of this group. I have a differentiated role as author. You also continue to function both as an individual and as a group member in the role of reader. We also have two other group members, Kelly and Richard. I speculate that they have joined our group to help us by taking up two other differentiated roles.

Kelly is in the role of the individual who has difficulty joining a group. Perhaps the process of joining evokes anxiety. If anxiety is the result of a conflict between a wish and a fear, then the anxiety about joining our group may involve a conflict between wanting the experience of attachment and belonging to a group coupled with the fear of losing individuality. Richard, on the other hand, is in the role of group member who has surrendered to the process of joining. When such group members belong to a dysfunctional group or family, mental health professionals frequently describe them as enmeshed or without boundaries. This description covertly loads shame into these group members, and the message with the shame is that needing to belong to a group and being willing to surrender one's individuality is disgusting and repulsive.

I offer you the following premise as an answer to how the group carries the message of recovery: by being a group. I further suggest that being a group entails three necessary conditions:

1. Each member of the group identifies with each of the other members and with each of the other group parts.
2. Each member speaks on behalf of the whole group, representing one of its parts.
3. The group maintains an ongoing awareness of and attention to its own process.

You might ask then, is a group of people drinking in a bar carrying the message of recovery? In order to answer this question, we must first define the members of this group. Certainly each person drinking, the bartender, and any other people present are all members of the group. Have we forgotten any group members? What about the alcohol? Is the alcohol acknowledged as a group member? Do the members of the group identify with the central role of alcohol in their group? Is alcohol given a voice with authority to speak on behalf of the group?

Contrast this group drinking in a bar with a group of alcoholics joined together in a meeting of Alcoholics Anonymous. Many newcomers to AA wonder how a group of alcoholics can stay sober while they spend so much time talking and thinking about alcohol. I suggest that in AA, alcohol achieves the distinction of being an honored group member. Indeed, without the existence of alcohol as a group member, the group could not have been formed in the first place. Each time a group member talks about his or her relationship with alcohol, the central role of alcohol in each member's life is acknowledged.

Contrast also the role of the sober alcoholic in a group of active drinkers with the role of an active drinker in a group of sober alcoholics. One sober alcoholic has the potential to seriously interfere with the denial of active drinkers. A possible explanation for this phenomenon is that the presence of a sober group member effortlessly breaks the group rule that alcohol goes unacknowledged in being universally consumed. The alcoholic who is not sober, but simply "going on the wagon," is understood by such a group to be weak. The group expects such a member to rejoin them in drinking as soon as this member is in control again. On the other hand, the active drinker receives a warm welcome by the group of sober alcoholics. The presence of the active drinker not only does not violate any group rules, but the group depends on its openness to new members for its continuing existence. These new members are often initially active drinkers.

Let us apply the criteria for how a group carries the message of recovery to our own group. First I ask myself, am I able to identify with each of the other members of this group and with each of the group's parts? I use the fact that I am writing at this moment as evidence that I identify myself with the author. I believe that I am identifying with you, the reader, as I consider how I can best convey to you this idea of a group carrying the message of recovery. I also believe that I am identifying with Richard in surrendering to the process of joining. I act in accordance with this identification by writing this book, but also, more significantly, by opening membership in the group to both Richard and Kelly. My identification with Kelly is more difficult. Here, in order to identify with Kelly, I must own my anxiety about joining the group. I must examine my use of lecturing to you or telling stories as a means of remaining distant and unattached to our group. I wonder how the rest of this group experiences the process of identifying with other group members.

I was wondering how long it would take you to ask that question. I was afraid I had lost my voice entirely. So I guess I can identify with your being the author in that I want to have a voice here, too. As I examine my anger and loneliness in relation to your long-winded soliloquy, I must be identifying with Kelly's isolation, what you call her anxiety about joining. And as much as I hate to admit it, because it tends to confirm your theory, I have the most trouble identifying with your silent reader, who seems to have no voice at all.

Why do you keep picking on the reader, Richard?

Why do you need to jump to the reader's defense? What do you have to say for yourself about this nasty business of identification?

As I have said here a million times before, identification is one of those words I hear all the time in AA, and I hate it. I will share an experience at a meeting, and some twit will chirp that she identifies with me. Then she will share some totally unrelated experience that convinces me that she did not understand a word I was saying. So I cannot really honestly say I identify with anyone here, except maybe I identify with the reader, because I know that I have to force myself to speak at AA meetings. If I were left to my own devices, I would spend all of my time reading, too, although my taste runs more to trashy mysteries than absurd books about groups and recovery. So I identify with my fantasy of the reader, curled up in bed reading this book in isolation. What I experience with you, Richard, would be envy rather than identification. I know that Dr. Roth loves you more than he loves me; after all, he just admitted it.

Kelly, he said that he had difficulty identifying with you . . .

Don't play stupid, Richard. If he really loved me, he would have no difficulty identifying with me.

Thank you, Kelly. I can hear that message clearly in my head: "My failure to identify is my failure to love." That message is a trap for me. If I identified with you perfectly, then I would have no resistance to joining the group, because I can more easily identify with the rest of the group. But since you have difficulty joining the group, if I pretend to have resistance I am not really identifying with you or loving you at all.

Now I ask you, gentle reader, if you are not totally lost in this last paradox, to embrace a paradox that may hit closer to home for you. Please find a pen, and consider writing the following sentence on the lines provided below: "In writing this sentence in this book, I am identifying with you, the author, by joining you in the activity of writing, and becoming a co-author with you."

_____

_____
_____
_____

So, have you written these lines? Whether or not you have done so, what feelings came up for you as you imagined putting your pen to this page? Perhaps you had any of these reactions:

1. Wow, I get to be co-author of this book!
2. I wrote the damn sentence, so what's the big deal?
3. Writing in books is improper, unmannered, and uncouth.
4. What does he want from me in making this stupid suggestion?
5. Why should I do this simply because he suggested it?
6. If I were going to write anything here, I would certainly write what I wanted!

If your only reaction resembles number one, you are clearly able to identify with me. However, if in joining me as co-author, you disparage your role as reader, you may have abandoned this role and failed to identify with this necessary part of our group. If you react more in line with number two, you probably identify more with Richard. In either case, you may share my difficulty in identifying with Kelly's reluctance to join me as an equal partner. Response number three is an indirect way of saying that wanting to join a group is shameful and pathetic.

Responses number four through six are all variations on the same theme: "I am an individual and I will not surrender my individuality to join a group." Response number four is a particularly tenacious paradox. This responder wants to be able to know what is going on in my head prior to joining with me, without identifying with me. Often the response is not phrased as honestly as this one; the responder is more polite and hides the contempt for the suggestion. The underlying process of this response is similar to a common form of denial in addiction: "I will not stop using until I understand why I am using." The trap here is that the addict may be blind to the motivation for becoming intoxicated as a result of the process of intoxication. All of the reasons for using may become painfully clear as feelings emerge in the process of recovery. Likewise, all of the justifications for remaining isolated may only reach the surface of awareness as a result of the process of joining.

Response number five is another version of my patient who takes the position: "I am only here because you invited me." Disavowal of one's own need to be connected renders any capacity to join ineffective and nonproductive. This disavowal is well illustrated by the common practice of court-mandated attendance at treatment groups and AA meetings for those convicted of driving while intoxicated. These individuals are clear from the outset that they resent being in treatment or in the AA group. The miracle of a group that carries the message of recovery, be it a Twelve-Step group or a therapy group, is that the group openly and unconditionally accepts the individual with any and all of the individual's resistance to joining. By accepting the resistance, the group opens a path to examining the unmanageability (see Chapter 4) associated with this chronic pattern of isolation. More important for the group's survival, the acceptance of this resistance liberates the group from engaging in a power struggle over whether the individual actually joins the group, and uses the resistance as part of the group's work in identifying similar resistance in each group member.

So, in case you have left the lines blank, and you are wondering if this act of rebellion means you have not really joined this group, I suggest that avoiding membership is not that easy. Whatever path you choose, if we are able to identify with one another's position, and authorize one another to speak (or not speak) from our own roles in our own voices, we are functioning as a group carrying the message of recovery. This principle has profound implications for treatment. The therapy group designed to provide court-mandated treatment for driving while intoxicated or driving under the influence can be a lethal experience for the naïve therapist, who is, unfortunately, typically the therapist assigned (like their mandated members) to lead such groups. Group members, explicitly, and the group therapist, implicitly, resent being forced into an unwanted experience of joining. Imagine how different the scenario becomes if the therapist can openly acknowledge all of the resentment that unites the group. Focusing on this resentment, and the alcohol that is used to control it, becomes a task that unites the group. What about getting group members to stop drinking? We may have difficulty admitting that no one involved in a court-mandated treatment comes to the group in order to stop drinking. What unites the group is a compulsion to enter into power struggles with authority. The posture of this group is basic assumption fight-flight, and only by harnessing this fight in the service of joining can the group carry the message of recovery. Therefore, returning to you, leaving those lines blank becomes a means of not joining only if I deny your membership, which you exercise by carrying the role of not writing. I have to ignore your steadfast loyalty to remaining in the role of reader in order to deny your membership in this way.

To conclude this thought experiment, I would like to congratulate anyone who wrote anything else on those lines above. If I were in the mode of being a total control freak, I could insist that if you use those lines that you do it my way. This control on my part would threaten the ability of our group to carry the message of recovery, because I would be treating our group as if anything of value of necessity emanates directly from me. Expressed in other words, I would be enforcing a culture in which basic assumption dependence (see Chapter 1) would create a pseudo-group. If, on the other hand, I can recognize that by writing something, indeed anything that emanates from you, you are joining me in the most authentic possible way, then I fully embrace our partnership. This attitude of acceptance, which is the foundation for an appreciation of powerlessness, will be described in Chapter 3. What I would like to emphasize here is that what a group creates, how a group responds, and where a group ventures is unknowable by any single member of the group. If I am being faithful to this vision of a group, then, aside from a very general outline based on the Twelve Steps, I do not know in advance where this book is taking us. The same ambiguity that governs what now appears in the blank lines above in your copy of this book also applies to what precedes and what follows.

Finally, I describe the third characteristic for the group carrying the message of recovery. Because each member identifies with all other group members, and because each member speaks on behalf of the whole group, representing one or more of its parts, the group maintains an ongoing awareness of and attention to its own process. This group conscience, this ability of the group to see itself and speak of itself, its actions, and its feelings, corresponds to our more usual understanding of individual consciousness. Group consciousness is exercised in much the same way as any other group function; at any given time one or more members of the group are in the role of maintaining awareness of how the group is functioning.

I offer here a model of group function, then, that parallels a more familiar model of the individual mind. A well-functioning individual mind has the capacity to attend to its internal and external environment at the same time that it engages in specific tasks. In order to accomplish this complex mixture of activities, we imagine that different "spaces" in the mind are responsible for these different activities. Whether we name these "spaces" id, ego, and superego or hippocampus, frontal lobe, and parietal lobe, we conceptualize these "spaces" as parts of the individual mind. If we imagine a group mind, in which individuals in the group assume responsibility for different tasks of the group, then we can see the group much like a single organism that functions effectively or in an impaired manner. A primary distinction between the human mind and the "minds" of other animals may be the human mind's capacity for self-awareness. This same distinction may be drawn between groups that support an awareness of their own process and groups that suppress this awareness in the service of maintaining their disease. This suppression of awareness would be what we generally call denial.

A major limitation in our thinking about denial is the characterization of denial in terms of content. Denial may be used to describe the alcoholic's lack of acceptance of suffering from a disease, as if the denial were about a fact relating to an individual. If denial of alcoholism is expressed as part of a dysfunctional group process, then this denial indicates the group's inability to be aware of the role that alcohol plays in its functioning in the here and now.

I believe that we now have possession of all the tools we need to understand how the group carries the message of recovery; this understanding is most succinctly stated in the Twelfth Step of the Twelve-Step programs (see Appendix A for the Twelve Steps of Alcoholics Anonymous). The Twelfth Step reads "Having had a spiritual awakening as the result of these Steps, we tried to carry this message to others, and to practice these principles in all our affairs." Let us examine this step one piece at a time. If we appreciate that the core of a spiritual awakening is the awareness of one's self and one's place in relation to the group (mankind), then we can accept that the direct result of this awareness by a group is that this group carries the message of recovery. That this awareness is a group, rather than an individual, phenomenon is seen in the use of the pronoun "we." The use of the word "tried" emphasizes that carrying the message is a process rather than an event. Those who still suffer include every member of the group, as well as anyone who might want to join the group. The commitment to practice the principles of recovery in all of our affairs makes explicit that recovery does not entail only abstinence from diseased behavior, but also the actual joining of a community in order to engage in roles determined by the community's needs and resources.

I have been bending your ears for a while now, and you have listened patiently. Are there any feelings or thoughts before we proceed to look at powerlessness and free association?

I was beginning to wonder whether I was still a member of this group. Maybe the reader is willing to listen to you drone on incessantly, but I thought the whole point of my coming here was to engage in real relationships. So what gives here?

I have been sitting here wishing I were dead. My cat has been sick, and I have not been able to sleep, my leg has been hurting more and more, and I am not getting any help from you at all.

I'm sure that Dr. Roth knows what he is doing, Kelly. And I feel so sorry that your cat is sick, that you are sleeping poorly, and that you still have pain in your leg.

Who asked you for an opinion, Bea? And since when were you invited to this group?

Hi, Bea. What a surprise! I missed you. It feels like the old group is getting back together again. Roth, you rascal, why didn't you tell me this would be a reunion? Except for your mysterious reader friend, it feels like the good old times. So what's new, Bea?

Well, I am facing a really big challenge in my recent marriage. And as difficult as it is, I want to thank the group for all of your support in helping me be able to be in this relationship.

Cut the sarcasm, Bea. And I hate it when you cozy up to Jeffrey this way. I find it really disgusting.

A little jealous, Kelly?

Go to hell, Richard. If Jeffrey loved me as much as he loves you, I wouldn't have to be jealous.

I think we are being insensitive here, guys. We are excluding the poor reader from our conversation. We have a history with one another and we are not letting the reader in on it.

So now you betray me, Bea! I have been holding the fort against Kelly's protecting the reader. If the reader wants to say something, the reader will just have to find a voice.

Hold on, Richard. As much as I hate her, maybe Bea has a point. I usually believe that Jeffrey suppresses my voice; maybe Jeffrey is suppressing the reader's voice as well.

Hey! This line of reasoning is not what I meant at all. Dr. Roth would never shut down anybody. He has never been anything but supportive of me. I am not always happy about being confronted by him, but he is consistently fair and honest. I was just wondering whether we were having a difficult time with this new member, the reader.

I would like to echo the sentiment of gratitude I hear from the group about our functioning as a recovering family. Therefore, I take seriously the questions from the group about the role of the reader in this group. I would like to seriously consider the question of how your voice, dear reader, emerges in this book. So before proceeding to the next chapter, I invite you to reflect on your feelings and thoughts thus far about being in this group, what role or roles you are playing, and most important, what forces may be interfering with your experience of having a voice in the proceedings.

Let me also remind you that if your choice has been to exercise your voice through silence, you have still made a choice. If we are serious about this being a group, then your choice about how to use your voice will reflect your relationship with me and the other members of this group. This experience of making choices and not being in control of the outcome or the meaning of these choices lies at the heart of powerlessness.

Chapter 3

Powerlessness and Free Association

I offer you the following meditation to illustrate our powerlessness over the outcome of our choices and the meaning of these choices:

Focus on your breathing. Take the next three breaths as deeply as you can. Notice that during these deep breaths you feel different; perhaps you have a little more energy. The next several breaths after the deep breaths are a little slower; you may feel different again; perhaps you are a little calmer. Your attention has wandered away from your breathing, which has become automatic again. Notice that you cannot let your attention wander and also monitor your breathing closely at the same time.

Breathing is one of the simplest examples of powerlessness. We are all powerless over breathing. Unless we dedicate some attention or awareness to breathing, we inspire and expire automatically. If we choose to focus on our breathing we can radically change its shape for brief periods of time. We can suspend our breathing for a period of minutes at the most; we can hyperventilate to the point of dizziness and pass out. After making these efforts to change our breathing, we resume our usual pattern of breathing within minutes of our efforts to change. When we resume this usual, automatic pattern our attention is free to attach to other activities. Our inability to let our minds wander while focusing on breathing is the foundation for breathing meditations, which are designed to offer an opportunity to let go of thinking by having all of our attention dedicated to breathing.

I suggest that our ability to focus, or narrow our attention, in the service of concentrating on one task is highly adaptive if not essential to our survival. Our ability, therefore, to sustain certain vital activities, like breathing, automatically and without consciousness supports our ability to focus our attention on other activities. Under ordinary circumstances, we do not need to hide the fact that we are breathing and we would not be inclined to deny that we are powerless over breathing.

Let us examine another physiological function that might seem at first glance to be quite analogous to breathing—eating. Some significant differences are immediately apparent. We breathe every five seconds, whereas we eat every several hours. The rhythmicity and volume of breathing is much more consistent than that of eating. These differences are probably a result of adaptations to the usually constant supply of oxygen as contrasted with highly variable supplies of food. Given these differences, the innate mechanisms of regulation of breathing and eating are remarkably similar. Over quite extensive periods of time, certainly weeks if not months or years, levels of oxygenation and nutrients in the blood are held remarkably constant. This regulation occurs without conscious intent in both cases.

Despite the automatic regulation of breathing and eating, we can choose to impair these functions with a variety of methods. Sufficient doses of alcohol, sedatives, or opiates will result in respiratory depression or collapse and death. Prolonged starvation will result in relatively quick depletion of the body's resources, suppression of the body's hunger mechanism, and ultimately death within a few months. Compulsive overeating will override the body's satiety mechanism and result in weight gain until the body suffocates in its own stored fat.

In taking actions that result in the impairment of automatic functions, we may develop an illusion of power and control. What we then mean by power is the ability to destroy ourselves. Here is the heart of the paradox of powerlessness:

I struggle for power and control over every aspect of my existence. I reject help from others because that would interfere with my illusions of control. If I do receive anything from outside of myself I convince myself that I manipulated and engineered the transaction. The illusion of manipulation is essential to maintain my belief in power and control.

This position contrasts with the following one:

I admit my powerlessness over every aspect of my existence. I ask for help from others with any task where I might develop the illusion of control. These tasks include anything that I am thinking about, anything that I am not doing automatically.

Does that mean you are also powerless over our interrupting you?

Give him a chance to develop his ideas on powerlessness, Richard. He was nice enough to invite us to join him here, so let's listen.

Damn it, Bea! This group is not about being nice. Besides, maybe we are powerless over when we participate and when we listen.

I wish you would all stop this mumbo jumbo about power- lessness. If I had lost control over anything, I had lost control over drinking. I stopped drinking, and I go to AA meetings ev- ery once in a while so I won't drink again. But what does that have to do with breathing or eating?

Funny that you should be asking that question, Kelly.

What are you talking about?

Well, as far as breathing is concerned, you cannot walk more than a block without becoming short of breath.

How can you make fun of a person who suffers from emphy- sema!

I am surprised that you are not being nice about this, Bea. Good for you. So Kelly, your emphysema has nothing to do with thirty years of smoking cigarettes?

From you or Dr. Roth I would expect such an attack. You know I stopped smoking a couple of years ago as part of Dr. Roth's treatment.

And since you stopped smoking, you have been obsessed with gaining weight.

Hey! You are treating me unfairly. I never told you that you could trot out my personal business here.

Complain to Roth. Maybe we are also powerless over divulging secrets.

Thanks for your help, group. I was feeling some fear about starting this chapter with a lecturette. I especially appreciate this segue into the topic of secrets.

See Richard! I told you Dr. Roth loves you more than he loves me.

I hope that I have not been keeping my partiality to Richard a secret. The cornerstones of Twelve-Step recovery are honesty, openness, and willingness. One frequently hears in Twelve-Step meetings that we are as sick as our secrets. We might assume that it is what we are hiding or keeping secret that makes us sick. I suggest that it is more significant *that we are hiding something* than whatever in particular we are hiding. What we are hiding, such as alcohol or drugs or compulsive eating, may kill us quickly or slowly. That we are hiding something isolates us from other people and kills our ability to participate most fully and meaningfully in the moment in the groups that we belong to.

Keeping secrets may entail hiding information or feelings from others or from ourselves. Hiding information is the more usual understanding of keeping secrets. We may more easily identify the person who drinks alone, hides liquor, and lies about lateness or absence as an alcoholic than the person whose social life revolves around bars. The group described drinking in a bar (Chapter 2) is also engaged in keeping a secret. This group does not conceal its drinking. No one in the group would deny that the group is consuming alcohol. The secret would be a process secret: no one in the group would admit that their primary goal in gathering together is to be socially isolated through intoxication.

Having to maintain secrets is a major stumbling block in being honest. I suggest that what we call honesty is the ability to speak one's mind, to share thoughts, feelings, and fantasies without restraining or suppressing oneself. The compulsion to maintain secrecy provides various rationalizations and justifications for not being honest and direct. Sometimes these rationalizations and justifications are based on fears of consequences to oneself of being honest, and sometimes they are based on the illusion that keeping the secret will altruistically protect someone else.

As therapists, we have a fancy name for honesty, which we call free association. Free association is the process of reporting thoughts, feelings, fantasies, dreams, jokes, and slips of the tongue without censorship or suppression. Free association demands spontaneity and freedom from secrets. We are not surprised then, that addicts have difficulty with free association. This difficulty may take two basic forms. One strategy is for the addict to avoid any thoughts that relate to the addiction. However, since the nature of addiction is that of an obsession that overrides all other aspects of life, the addict's attempt to freely report thoughts and feelings grinds to a halt every time an association leads to the addiction. If the therapist listens only to what is being reported, and does not notice what is being avoided, both addict and therapist may be complicit in a process secret. The story of my reluctant patient is a good example of a process secret in which the patient acts as if the treatment were a result of my invitation only.

Naturally, if the addict suspends all attempts at hiding the addiction, free association inevitably and inexorably circles around the addiction. The one-dimensional experience of the addict's life achieves a remarkably accurate representation as every thought, feeling, and fantasy leads to the addiction. Ironically, while the therapist may listen for years to an addict avoid all discussion of the addiction, when the addict is honestly able to talk only about the addiction, the therapist may conclude that the addict is untreatable. The therapist who assumes that the addiction can be controlled by understanding all of the associations to the addiction becomes increasingly frustrated by the addict's inability to talk or think about anything other than the addiction. The therapist engages in a covert power struggle with the addict in the mistaken belief that the meaning of the addiction can be determined without admitting that both the addict and the therapist are powerless over the disease process.

How does this process of free association appear in groups? If we accept the model of a group mind as introduced in Chapter 2, then we can describe a group that is able to report its thoughts, feelings, and fantasies without censorship or suppression.

That's ridiculous. I have been listening to your intellectual pandering to the reader about powerlessness and free association and I have been suppressing my rage about you ignoring me. This group shows no indication of free association.

Bravo, Kelly. Thank you for not leaving me alone in monitoring Roth's intellectualizing. But give the devil his due. The fact that you were able to interrupt him is an indication that we as a group are associating freely.

I am getting dizzy, Richard. Did you just defend Dr. Roth? I thought that was my job.

This group mind engaged in the process of free association may be capable of both attending to some external task and also monitoring its own function. When I am able to be respectful and grateful for the work of this group, I can observe the members of the group transacting relationships with each other and with me. These relationships support each of us in examining what roles we play here, how these roles are adaptive and how these roles may constrict or constrain us.

For example, this group lovingly confronts me on my intellectualization. If I recognize that intellectualization is something that I do, that I am powerless over it, and that it may interfere with my ability to associate freely, then I experience this group's confrontation as an opportunity to attach rather than defensively withdraw, rationalize, justify, or counterattack. Likewise, if the group elects one of its members to share an endless chain of associations connected to an addiction, I hope to be able to embrace this expression of powerlessness. I need to let go of my intellectual compulsion to understand what motivates the addiction in order to participate in appreciating and feeling the impact of the group's powerlessness over a process that is being voiced by one or more of its members.

I must be the most despicable person ever to have existed. I resent the fact that you ignore me. I resent you for having put me in this group. I resent your not protecting me from Richard. I resent you for loving Richard and not loving me. I resent having to deal with Bea's saccharine adoration of you.

Great Fourth-Step work, Kelly! Oops, I think Roth was waiting for a discussion of the Fourth Step until Chapter Seven.

I find it strange that you of all people, Richard, would be worried about Dr. Roth's agenda.

Thanks, Bea, you're right.

It's not fair for you to support me in whining, Richard. Here I am working up a head of steam and you knock the wind right out of me.

I am grateful for the group's help in our examination of powerlessness. You have an impressive recognition of your powerlessness over the roles you play here: Richard in monitoring my performance in my role as author, Kelly in carrying the group's resentment and resistance to joining, Bea in protecting me from the group's aggression, and you, the reader, in silently attempting to make sense of the confusion. I also hear the group poignantly describing the experiences of powerlessness. These experiences include being vulnerable to exposure and attack, having little or no control over impulses, being subject to unexpected intense feelings such as rage, grief, terror, panic, and shame and becoming completely confused, disoriented, dizzy, and unable to breathe. Small wonder that admitting our powerlessness by associating freely is not a popular activity.

There you go again, making fun of me. I resent your flippant attitude and your total lack of compassion for me.

I'm glad that Roth's intellectual diatribe has not interfered with your inventory work.

Stop supporting me, Richard. Do you want me to have to shift my rage from Roth to you?

If you directed your rage at me, at least I would have a more intimate experience of being connected to you. Right now I see you engaged in endless exclusive foreplay with Roth.

Why would you bring up sex here, Richard? Kelly's ragging on Dr. Roth doesn't seem to be at all romantic.

So up until your recent marriage, what did you know about romance? And if Kelly were young enough to still be on the rag, her PMS'ing at Roth would be quite sexual indeed.

Are you accusing me of being seductive, Richard?

Since when is being seductive an accusation, rather than an affirmation? Maybe I'm envious of your attentions to Roth.

You vicious backstabber, I'm the only one who gets to be jealous.

I would like to check in with you, the reader, and to inquire about your thoughts, feelings, reactions, and fantasies in connection with our discussion of powerlessness and free association. I pose what may seem to be simple questions: Can you imagine Kelly, Richard, Bea, you, and me sitting in a circle of chairs in a room? Do you place yourself outside the room looking in at the rest of us, inside the room but outside of the circle, or sitting in the circle with the group? Maybe you imagine yourself at the center of the circle with the rest of us looking at you or perhaps you put me or another member in the center. Let us map out some of the possibilities (you will be X and the rest of us O):

X

O	X	X	O O	O X
O O	O	O O	X	O
O	O O	O O	O O	O O
	O			

Now assign a value to each of these possibilities, giving the number one to the configuration that best describes your experience or fantasy of how you relate to the group and number five to the configuration that least describes this relationship.

I hope that you can imagine a number of possible responses to my request. You may refuse to engage in this exercise entirely, and if you do make some explicit rank ordering, you have many different ways to accomplish this. With respect for your capacity for insight into which particular choice you made, I will leave to you the examination of why you chose to respond or not, and how you responded if you did. What I want to draw your attention to is the possibility that you are powerless over the choice that you made, and that this choice may reflect prior experiences in other groups, including your family of origin.

I cannot know with certainty about your reaction, but in my experience many people have difficulty with the idea that they are powerless over the roles they assume in the groups they join. For those of us acculturated to individualism, our assumption is that we are in control of our transactions with other people. You are now in a position to identify closely with the addict who stands at the threshold of recovery. Every fiber of the addict's being screams, "I am an individual. I can fix my problems by myself. I do not need a group. I am not a member of a group. I will not join a group." Such is the intensity of reaction to the experience of powerlessness. Therefore I want to be sensitive to the possibility that you might be revisiting the question of whether you are indeed a member of this group. I assure you that you would not be alone.

While many addicts reject Twelve-Step groups on the basis of a distortion of the concept of higher power as God, I suspect a more genuine accounting for their reluctance stems from our intense anxiety over admitting powerlessness. Review for a moment the exercise at the beginning of this chapter on our powerlessness over breathing. I hope that we agree that breathing is an automatic function that we can make temporary adjustments to by focusing all of our attention in a concentrated manner. Now consider that the role you play in our group is just as automatically carried out as your breathing, that you may be able to execute temporary adjustments with focused attention, but that as you go back to focusing on anything else, including what I am writing to you at this moment, that you automatically resume the role you have adapted to.

Now you might object that I have created the role you are in. I am, after all, the author of this book, so you might accurately assert that I have a major role in determining the direction that we take. You might also accurately assert that you would be highly unlikely to be examining the role that you play in this relationship if not for my stubborn insistence that we pay attention to you. I suggest that the crux of the matter here is that you have choices about how you exercise your role as reader. Admittedly these choices are largely internal to you. I have offered you some opportunities to make these choices explicit, including when I invited you in the preface to be open to your skepticism and also not to read this book alone, when I suggested in Chapter 1 to give voice to your doubt about joining this group, when I offered you an opportunity to write with me in Chapter 2, and when I presented in this chapter some alternative ways for you to view your position in this group. I hope I have demonstrated to you that, despite the constraints inherent in your role as reader, you have considerable freedom in how you play this role. I then propose to you that this freedom entails two consequences: first, I am powerless over how you choose to exercise your role as reader, and second, you are powerless over how you exercise this role. Again, please remember that your powerlessness does not mean you cannot modify your role over brief periods of time. I am simply suggesting that the role you adopt here is determined by a number of factors, some of which you may have examined in other contexts such as therapy or Twelve-Step groups and some of which you may never have had reason or opportunity to examine. Perhaps as I acknowledge that, since I have never written this particular book before, I am powerless over how I am exercising my role as author, neither of us needs to remain isolated in our powerlessness over how we relate to each other here. In this way we might appreciate the wisdom of the first part of the first step of the Twelve-Step programs, "We admitted we were powerless . . ."

Are you finished kissing up to the reader?

Oh my God, Richard! Have you taken on the role of being jealous?

Chapter 4

Unmanageability and Resistance

The unmanageability of addiction is frequently attributed to some specific form of intoxication. Thus the alcoholic's unmanageability is portrayed as drunkenness, the cocaine addict's unmanageability as stimulant rush, and the opiate addict's unmanageability as dreamy euphoria. These attributions consolidate the characteristics of addiction around the drug of choice and ignore the deeper impact of addiction on the addict's life. If we understand addiction as a disease of isolation that emerges in what Philip Flores (1997) has described as an attachment disorder, then the particular form of intoxication chosen by the addict might relate to what the addict needs in order to remain isolated. This distinction between the drug of choice and the disease of addiction has been described by members of Alcoholics Anonymous as their suffering not only from the effect of alcohol but more from the effect of the "ism." Recovering alcoholics may point out that the "ism" for them is an abbreviation for "*I sponsor myself*," thus highlighting the centrality of isolation in their disease.

We have seen in Chapter 3 how the addict's secrecy and inability to be honest about the addiction leads to impaired attachment to anyone else. This loss of the addict's capacity to be authentic, to have the addict's "insides" match the "outsides," may be the most significant index of unmanageability of addiction. Let me illustrate this principle with another story.

Another Story

An addict was nearing the depths of despair as his addiction had resulted in the loss of his job and deterioration of his marriage. He realized that the only escape from his miserable downward spiral was to commit suicide. His only reservation was that he really cared about his wife, and he wanted to spare her the suffering of losing her husband. Fortunately, the addict was an

incredibly gifted scientist who was prominent in the field of robotics. So he
manufactured an exact double of himself; the only detectable difference between the robot and him was that instead of a heartbeat the robot produced
a soft whirring in its chest.

On the night that he had planned to commit suicide, the scientist carried
the robot to the bed that he shared with his wife. His eyes welled up with
tears as he watched his wife sleeping peacefully, and then he carefully laid
the robot in bed next to her. He was overwhelmed by a sudden desire for a final moment of contact with his wife before he killed himself. As he impul-
sively put his ear on her chest, he was horrified to hear only a soft whirring.

Illusion is the heart of unmanageability. The addict's resistance in
treatment inevitably connects to a compulsion to preserve illusions,
particularly the illusion of control. If the addict is in control of the disease, then the addict does not need to work on a meaningful attachment to a work group, a family group, or a therapy group.

*Kelly, since you seem to recognize that you have been carrying the
role of being jealous, and you indicated that Richard may have taken
up this role for you, perhaps we might examine your past jealousies
in relation to me.*

**I don't know. It has been such a long time since you paid any
attention to me, I am not sure I can trust your motives in this.**

*Damn it, Kelly. You bitch incessantly about Roth ignoring you, and now
when he offers to work with you, you would turn him down?*

Thank you for questioning my motives. I have been thinking about
a diagnostic category that is no longer in use. It was called alcoholic
delusional jealousy. The diagnosis described a condition in which an
alcoholic would become convinced that the spouse was having an affair. One way of approaching this diagnosis was to assume that alcohol exerted some pharmacological effect on the brain that stimulated
thoughts or delusions of infidelity. One problem with this approach is
that delusional jealousy may appear in a spouse who is not drinking.
So on the next revision of diagnostic categories, alcoholic delusional
jealousy became known simply as delusional jealousy. In my opinion, the revision was unwarranted, except that I might have extended
the alcoholism part to include any addiction. I suggest that in (alcoholic) delusional jealousy, one or both spouses are invariably addicts.
In practice, the addict is engaged in an affair with the addiction. The

alcoholic is frequently described by the spouse as married to the bottle; the workaholic is described as married to the job. So, ironically, the jealousy is really not all that delusional. In the cases in which the addict has the delusion that the spouse is having an affair, sometimes this delusion may be merely a projection of the addict's affair with the addiction. Some spouses do become alienated enough in the face of neglect from the addict that an affair is seen as the only way to experience a minimal connection to the world outside. Many relationships in which an addiction is active could be described by the metaphor of two robots sleeping in the same bed.

Okay, Roth, are you suggesting that we are all behaving like robots here?

Richard, are you taking all this a little too personally?

Will you ever stop defending Jeffrey, Bea?

You are all raising interesting questions. In relation to the idea that the members of this group are behaving like robots, I have wondered if the reader, not being as familiar with you as I am, might have doubts about your reality or authenticity. Then again, some doubts might exist about the reality or authenticity of the unseen reader.

Let us extend our examination of diagnostic categories to consider an informal category that has never been validated, which is the "addictive personality" or "alcoholic personality." Organizing addiction as a specific personality defect perpetuates the assumption that addiction is a disease of the individual rather than the family group. Not surprisingly, then, personality studies have invariably failed to correlate specific uniform personality traits to addiction. One unspoken implication of these personality studies has been to isolate a specific group of people who would then be at risk for addiction, allowing the rest of us to breathe a sigh of relief that we were not affected with the shameful condition. If, on the other hand, addiction were an equal opportunity disease, we might all be powerless over suffering from this disease, particularly if the disease affects the group rather than the individual.

If we accept the concept of addiction as a family disease, then we would not necessarily expect this disease to produce uniform effects in the individual. Assuming that as individuals we are endowed with a substantial diversity of talents, competencies, and vulnerabilities, then a disease designed to interfere with attachment might need to adapt itself to the specific characteristics of its host. This model for a disease adapting to its host has been demonstrated for diseases with more acceptable biological bases, such as viral infections.

Imagine now the plight of a child born to parents who are locked in a struggle with an addiction. Absent any other children, we would see a group consisting of three explicit members: father, mother, and child, and one member whose presence would be disavowed, the addiction. To the extent that alternative models of relationships were not available, the child's model for attachment would tend to be the pattern provided by its impaired parents. The child who learns these dysfunctional patterns early might be predisposed to repeating these patterns throughout the rest of its life. This repetition may include engaging in the overt addictive behaviors modeled by one or both parents or finding a partner to enact the addictive behaviors in order for the adult child to be the enabler. As this adult child compulsively repeats either pattern of addictive or enabling behavior, the illusion is maintained that this time the adult child can control the trauma of being disconnected from the family group and achieve mastery over the experience of isolation.

The compulsion to repeat or reenact self-destructive behavior patterns during the active phase of addiction defines both our powerlessness over the disease and its unmanageability. *Because we are powerless over addiction, these same dysfunctional patterns may be creatively reenacted without the burden of intoxication during treatment and recovery, particularly in a group.* The trauma of growing up in the addicted family shows as much variation and diversity as the addictions themselves. Some of the more obvious and dramatic traumata include sexual abuse and physical violence; less obvious traumata range from emotional abuse and abandonment to more subtle traumata such as role reversals in which children become caretakers for their parents. The presence of an obvious trauma such as sexual abuse does not preclude a subtler trauma such as role reversal. Because the role reversals frequently produce children who are highly competent caretakers, denial about their childhood trauma is often the most difficult to confront.

I need to talk about the unmanageability in my life.

Hi, Warren. Welcome back. Where have you been?

How did you know that we were listening to Dr. Roth talk about unmanageability?

Hi, guys. Sorry I have not been here in a while. My not being here is probably part of my unmanageability.

What's happening?

Why do we drop everything to pay attention to Warren when he shows up? I guess his stories are just more interesting than mine.

Actually, Kelly, I have had the same question. Although I am grateful that the group makes space for me, I wonder sometimes if you are patronizing me because I am the token black member of the group. Of course, when I am accusing the group in my head of defending against its racism, I question whether Inner Nigger is at work.

I don't think the reader is familiar with Inner Nigger.

I get so enraged at your incessant caretaking, Bea! What do you really care about the reader? You are just trying to impress Dr. Roth!

I'm sorry, reader. I do hold myself accountable not to marginalize other people. Inner Nigger is the part of my mind that keeps me isolated as a black man. Inner Nigger, whom I call IN, tells me never to trust anyone who is white. IN also tells me that all black men are dogs, including me, and that all black women are whores or bitches. IN tells me that my sharing this information with a bunch of white folks makes me the world's most despicable Oreo.

So what are you sitting on? You said you wanted to talk about something.

Yeah. Well you all know, except maybe for the reader, that I have been working my way up the city bureaucracy. I have no idea why they let a dumbass nigger who squeaked through an undistinguished college and graduated from a shit law school make it this far up in city government.

Where is that self-abuse coming from?

Cut it out, Richard. We both know it's IN. Anyway, I'm in deep shit now. I have just been promoted again, and now my boss is a black woman. I cannot get the idea out of my head that the bitch is coming on to me. Of course, IN says if I were a real man, I'd screw her and get it over with. But I think that if I did screw her, IN would be all over me about how I was now her sex slave.

Maybe that has something to do with your sleeping with your mother after your father died of pancreatitis.

Duh. You know what, Bea? If IN were a white woman, I think you would fit the bill to a T.

Thank you, Warren and group, for helping me address another relevant diagnostic category, post-traumatic stress disorder (PTSD).

Those who suffer from PTSD complain of recurrent intrusive thoughts, feelings, and memories called flashbacks, in which they experience being back in a past traumatic incident and reliving it. They may also give a history of attempts to avoid these flashbacks, usually by identifying cues or triggers that evoke their flashbacks, and then avoiding their triggers. This strategy of avoidance may be successful for a while, until or unless the affected person's life becomes constricted through avoidance to the point of being unmanageable. Supportive therapy for PTSD may include medications to suppress the intense feelings that accompany flashbacks.

Consider for a moment the possibility that the disordered part of PTSD is the avoidance rather than the flashbacks themselves. Two features of flashbacks might explain the urgency involved in avoiding them. First, flashbacks typically involve rather intense feelings, including terror and panic. Second, and equally important, the flashbacks and feelings are out of the control of the sufferer, and they may arise seemingly out of nowhere, repeatedly, defying any attempt by the sufferer to keep them at bay. In short, the person afflicted with PTSD is powerless over having flashbacks. I suggest, though, that despite the overwhelming quality of the feelings, these feelings alone do not generate unmanageability. The disorder relies on attempts to control these feelings to achieve its pathogenic effect.

Pushing this idea just a step farther, imagine that the pathogenesis of PTSD involves the storage of feelings that could not be directly experienced at the time of the original trauma (not an original idea of mine). Then the flashbacks might represent the sufferer's attempt to experience these intense feelings in a safe environment. A safe environment refers to a physical and emotional place where feelings can be shared and expressed in all of their intensity without the need for internal or external control.

In this context, unmanageability might be defined as the compulsion to repeat prior trauma under conditions that lead to continued repetition rather than experiencing and letting go of the feelings attached to the trauma. We might then conceptualize addiction as the creation of conditions within a family or group in which the group repeats the trauma for those in authority and may initiate trauma for those born into the system (the children). One necessary condition for the addiction is that safeguarding the secret of the addiction takes precedence over the right of the group or family to be honest and open in expressing feelings.

Well, Dr. Roth, I believe that you have painted yourself into a corner here. You are the authority in our group, and I have been traumatized by your withholding of love from me. I feel enraged about your neglect of me, and I cannot share these feelings because you clearly are not hearing me.

You raise an interesting point, Kelly, although as usual you get lost in your self-pity. So, Roth, how do you account for any work taking place in a therapy group if we are powerless over repeating your trauma?

Please, Richard, let's not get into blaming Dr. Roth for our problems.

Guys, you can really do better work than this. If we are going to crucify Dr. Roth, let's do it honestly. Richard, you told me outside of group that Dr. Roth recently owned up to his use of intellectualization as a defense. You even confessed privately that you were impressed by his candor.

I guess I'm busted. You've got me on that one.

So if we are not expecting Dr. Roth to be God, and he can acknowledge his own shortcomings, perhaps we are not all victims of a dysfunctional system

here. Now don't any of you hold me to anything that I just said, because IN is already on my ass about "Uncle Tomming" Dr. Roth.

Thank you for your support in holding me accountable here. First I want to admit that I have not given an adequate description of authority yet, so any attempt to describe how group therapy or recovery works would have to be incomplete. I commit to you that we will commence with an examination of authority in the group in Chapter Five and address the issues raised by Kelly. I am also impressed that Warren and Richard anticipate my wish to look at special relationships as part of surrender in Chapter Six.

Chapter 5

The Higher Power of the Group
As a Symbol of Authority

Many of us understand authority as power held by someone else that may be given to us under certain conditions. We may experience this authority who is the source of power as benevolent, malignant, or apathetic to us. We assume without even realizing that we have made an assumption that the power residing in authority originates in this authority and that we play no role in whether we share this power and how we share it.

We touched the issue of authority briefly in our relationship of me as author and you as group members in Chapter 1. I suggested there (page 3) that if you authorize me to offer you some useful experience about groups, you might want my attention focused on our task. I suggest at this point that our task is to investigate the nature of authorization in groups in general and the experience of authorization in this group in particular. I would like to begin our investigation by challenging the assumption that power originates in authority.

If we use our most immediate example of authorization, which is your *author*ization of me as *author* of this book, we can develop two contrasting hypotheses about how I acquired my *author*ity. Again, in Chapter 1, when we examined how I came to write this book, I suggested that the attachments I have to editor, publisher, colleagues, friends, and family might *author*ize and *empower* me to engage with you right now. I also stated that I need you to read this book in order for me to write it. Perhaps you want to argue this point. Would you suggest that I could theoretically have written this book without any readers at all? I would then have to confront you with paradoxes on two counts: first, you are at this moment reading this book, and second, arguing with me and giving suggestions to me are indications that we are indeed attached as reader and author.

Let us then develop these two contrasting hypotheses. The first hypothesis is that I have the authority to write this book because I have a contract with my publisher and I have guidance from my editor. Under this hypothesis, I presumably receive this authority because of my competence, success, prestige, vanity, or family connections to publisher and/or editor. Depending on how you experience my exercising my authority, you may have a different fantasy about how I acquired it. If you experience me as benevolent, you might assume my authority was granted due to my competence; if malignant, you might attribute my authority to family connections; if apathetic, you might imagine me as driven by vanity or prestige. Notice that according to this first hypothesis, my authorization is a done deal. I have this authorization, it is mine, I own it, and it belongs to me. All of this is assumed to be true before you even set your eyes on the book cover.

The second hypothesis relies on an astonishingly simple, elegant, and yet easily lost concept: I receive the authority to write this book as a process, one moment at a time as you read the words that I have written. According to this hypothesis, my authority to write depends only on my availability to attach to you, the reader. Therefore, I do not have exclusive ownership of this authority. Authority belongs to us collectively; you give your authorization to me in order for me to write and in order for you to read. The moment you cease to authorize me, I am no longer an author in your life. You are free to give me authority until the end of this chapter, put down the book for a year and then reauthorize me by picking up this book again after that time. Note that this hypothesis does not allow you to be a victim of my authority since my authority is not *over* you; on the contrary, my authority is yours to give to me or withhold from me.

We have arrived at another crossroads. We met our first challenge in Chapter 1 when I asked you to consider the possibility that in reading this book you are joining a group with me. I emphasize here that I cannot prove to you that you have actually become a member of a group. You may or may not believe that you are a group member. I do insist that if you admit that you have joined this group, then we as a group are subject to our powerlessness over how we function as a group and that whatever attempt we make to control the function of our group will generate unmanageability. I hope that I have demonstrated these aspects of our group functioning in Chapters 3 and 4.

I now suggest that we consider adopting our second hypothesis: you are responsible as reader for my authorization. I cannot prove this one to you either. You may choose to believe that you are authorizing me or that you are irrelevant to the process of authorization. I will now further insist that if you believe that you are authorizing me, then you will have joined the group in a much more powerful manner. You will have joined in the creation of a group mind whose sum is greater than the sum of its parts: you and I and the rest of the group. In order to see that this group mind works as a unit, you have to believe that this group mind exists, and that we share equally in creating this group mind by giving our authorization for its creation.

The second step of the Twelve-Step programs reads "Came to believe that a Power greater than ourselves could restore us to sanity." This step is widely misinterpreted as an indication that the Twelve-Step Programs are essentially religious in orientation and function. In most religious contexts, ultimate authority is vested in one or more deities called God(s). The religion assumes our first hypothesis to be true, that God(s) has absolute authority as an intrinsic characteristic of Godhood. Each religion maintains some set of characteristics attributed to its God(s), which becomes part of its theology. Belief in and adherence to this theology defines membership in the religion.

Imagine a heretical alternative to this interpretation of the Second Step. What if this step suggests (in accord with our second hypothesis) that precisely the process of believing constitutes the authorization of a power greater than ourselves? In this scenario, we have no need for a defined theology or dogma; that we believe is of importance, so what in particular we choose to believe in becomes a subject for examination without prejudice. Consistent with this understanding of the Second Step is an established tradition within the Twelve-Step programs that each individual in recovery is free to define a Higher Power to suit individual needs and preferences.

Using this framework gives us another way to understand the story of my reluctant patient (Chapter 1, page 5) and "Another Story" (Chapter 4, page 39). My patient did not believe that she had come to me for help, and she was therefore unable to authorize me to help her. The husband in "Another Story" did not believe that he was a vital ingredient in forming a relationship, and therefore he did not notice that his wife had already left him.

By admitting powerlessness over the addiction and by admitting that continuing authorization of the addiction leads to unmanageability, the addict acknowledges a pattern of behavior in which the addiction has become a power greater than oneself. In many cases the addict has not had very much, if any, experience of any benevolent authority. The Second Step simply posits that the process of authorization *could* result in a more manageable life. If the addict does not believe that life could be more manageable, then the addict cannot authorize anything outside of the addiction to make life more manageable. Recovering addicts may explain their membership in a Twelve-Step program saying "My best thinking got me here."

I guess we have authorized you to go on a particularly lengthy intellectual binge, Dr. Roth.

Yeah. Maybe you qualify for the newest Twelve-Step program for compulsive talkers, On-and-on-Anon.

Long time no see, Leslie.

You should talk, Warren, the way you come and go.

I don't see how disregarding what Dr. Roth is saying can help us to authorize him.

Why should I authorize Dr. Roth when he won't even talk to me? We have just wasted the last several pages watching Dr. Roth cozy up to the reader and ignore me completely.

But Kelly, cut Dr. Roth some slack. I can understand him flirting with the reader. Actually, I think the reader is kind of cute myself.

You are nuts, Leslie. Do we have to watch you again now, falling in love with yet another unavailable partner?

Butt out, Kelly. If you are not interested in the reader, at least let me make my play. I like the mysterious silent types. The reader is paying attention to me, and the reader doesn't bore me to death like Roth here.

Leslie, I hope you understand that I am telling you this out of my love for you. Even taking Kelly's jealousy into consideration, you hardly know the reader well enough to start a romance.

Bea, I am surprised at you. I think we know a lot about the reader by now. After all, the reader has stuck with this insane group up to now. And imagine the reader's patience. None of the rest of us has managed to be able to listen quietly without chiming in at least occasionally.

I need to be explicit here that I have introduced Leslie into the group with malice aforethought. In case you have decided that you know Leslie's gender, let me alert you that Leslie's gender is purposefully ambiguous. I have used my authority in this group to add members in such a way as to maintain balance with respect to gender. The reader's gender is also ambiguous. So I suggest now that Leslie's gender matches the gender of the reader's choice of romantic partner.

You are a dog, Roth. You are setting up a match between Leslie and the reader.

I don't know if that's necessarily true, Richard. Dr. Roth is not powerful enough to control our sexual feelings. Maybe he is merely creating possibilities for sexual interaction. And given my propensity for winding up in bed with the women who flirt with me, maybe I need some practice in group learning alternative methods of responding to those situations.

You know, Warren, sometimes your capacity to kiss Roth's ass exceeds even our friend, Bea.

I resemble that remark.

You all disgust me. And what's worse, I know that I envy your ability to flirt with each other.

Indeed, flirtation is the freedom to imagine attaching to someone or something outside of oneself.

So all of you should be grateful for my return. Otherwise without me you would all be hopelessly stuck in your narcissism.

Better be careful with that index finger, Leslie. When it points at us, the other three fingers point back at you.

Perhaps the most important implication for group psychotherapy with recovering addicts of these two hypotheses about authorization is how each of them determines a different stance for the therapist.

The first hypothesis asserts that authority belongs to the therapist because of some characteristics intrinsic to the therapist. Both group members and therapist alike are susceptible to equating this intrinsic authority to power. The therapist has the power in this scenario to determine diagnosis, duration of treatment, when the person becomes abstinent and stops practicing the addiction and the agenda of what is talked about in treatment.

In contrast, if we adopt the second hypothesis, in which authorization is a mutual process among therapist and group members, the therapist is forcefully confronted with powerlessness over diagnosis, duration of treatment, continued practice of an addiction and agenda of group therapy sessions. You may wish to review Chapter 3 at this point to assist in our work of integrating authorization with powerlessness. I would like to examine each of the previously mentioned aspects of the group therapist's role in turn as it relates to the group therapist's powerlessness.

Let us start with the issue of diagnosis. The diagnosis is usually related to the person's presenting problem, which is both the ticket to entering therapy and also potentially subject to change. Unless the therapist is cast in the role of omniscient authority, we might imagine that new aspects of the presenting problem emerge in the course of the therapeutic relationship. The possibility of changing the presenting problem is, after all, what the person enters treatment in order to accomplish. Yet many people seem surprised that the problem(s) that drove them to seek help emerge in the helping relationship itself. This phenomenon of the person's difficulties showing up in relationship to the treatment has been called transference in the psychoanalytic model, and we will examine transference in greater detail in Chapter 6.

If I, as a group therapist, let go of my compulsion to immediately understand the person who comes to me for help, then I am not driven to establish a definitive diagnosis. As I admit my powerlessness over being able to enter into anyone else's mind, I become open to negotiating with the person about what we believe the problem is and how we might approach this problem together. In this way we define by our behavior a model for this person to authorize me as a therapist. When we are working together on preparing for this person to become a group member, the central issue is how we negotiate together how we will authorize the group to work.

One incredible benefit of group therapy is the amount of information that becomes explicit in the interactions among group members and group therapist. Here again, the powerlessness of the group therapist over how much information surfaces, and the rate at which it emerges is of paramount importance. If the complexity of a dyadic relationship is daunting, imagine one or two orders of magnitude greater complexity in a group; then we can more easily appreciate the reticence many therapists experience in relation to doing group therapy.

One obstacle for the neophyte group therapist is the attempt to establish a diagnosis before the person enters the therapy group. This obstacle often shows up in the form of exclusion criteria: those classes of people for whom membership in the group is considered undesirable. Ironically, alcoholics and addicts are frequently on this list of those excluded from general psychotherapy groups. If we allow diagnostic information to develop in parallel with authorization, then we can celebrate with our group members the increasing clarity each of them receives about their diagnosis (or diagnoses). This process of discovery is an explicit part of recovery in the Twelve-Step programs; the First Step does not read "I admitted that you were powerless." Group therapy can be an opportunity for addicts to find their own evidence of their own disease. The therapist and other group members inevitably hold up a mirror for the addict to see the addiction, but the final decision about diagnosis is still in the hands of the person who initiated the process of authorizing the therapy.

Continuing with the question of duration of treatment, we enter even more controversial waters. I suspect that in order to address this question I will need to tackle a delicate subject head on. This subject is the widespread notion that therapy or Twelve-Step programs replace one symptom or addiction with another symptom or addiction. In the case of therapy, some critics accuse the therapist of substituting a "sick" dependency on the therapist for whatever problem the person complained of originally. With Twelve-Step programs, like-minded detractors argue that those people in Twelve-Step recovery are simply addicted to meetings. If we return to the basic definition of addiction, which refers to a disease process necessarily entailing both powerlessness and unmanageability, then we see that while the recovering addict may indeed be powerless over a need for Twelve-Step meetings, this need for meetings usually makes life more manageable. We need not be surprised that some resourceful addicts become compulsive about attending meetings, attempting unwittingly to transform their recovery into a disease.

Right on! I mean, thanks Dr. Roth. When I first started going to meetings of Adult Children of Alcoholics, IN was all over my ass about how could I betray my daddy by letting anyone else know about the drinking and infidelity in my family. One meeting was too many. But I was a tortured soul, and when I didn't buckle under to the demands of IN that I stop going to meetings right away, I started to hear a different message. This voice said that I was insincere in my requests for help, that if I were serious about this recovery business I would be going to more meetings, that I should already have a sponsor and that my laziness in this recovery business was just one more indication of what a low-life I am. I am really grateful that you pointed out to me that this voice could be a disguise for IN.

We obviously need to do more work on your kissing up to Dr. Roth.

Thanks, IN.

So once again we have an opportunity as therapists to embrace our powerlessness, this time in the area of duration of treatment. I do not decide when a person chooses to ask me for help; I cannot decide whether or not this person will authorize me as a therapist, and therefore I cannot know with certainty how long a person stays in treatment. My powerlessness does not excuse me from my commitment to rigorous honesty. If I believe that I am limited in my ability to be of service, I need to make these limitations explicit at the outset of treatment. If I see that we have reached an impasse during treatment, I need to address the block directly and own my part of it as best I can.

Well you sure as hell have not owned your part of my being stuck. I have done everything you have suggested. I gave up alcohol, my tranquilizers, my laxatives, and my cigarettes and I am more miserable now than I have ever been my whole life. And my leg hurts so badly I think sometimes I should have it amputated.

You have been trying so hard to do all of these things by yourself, Kelly. I have invited you to come to Overeaters Anonymous with me to get support for recovering from your laxative abuse.

Bea, I don't trust you farther than I can spit. You just say these things to get closer to Dr. Roth. You don't care about me. None of you cares about me. Except maybe Richard. And Warren, I guess you have been kind to me.

One of the greatest challenges that I face as a therapist is that I am constantly seeing myself more clearly. With heightened clarity I become aware of mistakes that I have made. For example, early in my relationship with Kelly I jumped into attempting to rescue you.

Yes, that was when I really felt that you loved me.

When I was able to see that I was trying to work a program of recovery for you, I let go of pushing you.

That's your euphemistic way of saying you abandoned me.

Thank you for this segue to an examination of abstinence.

Ironically, abstinence has two separate specialized meanings in the fields of addiction treatment and psychoanalysis. In recovery from addiction, abstinence refers to not engaging in the compulsive behavior that characterized the addiction. Abstinence may be confused with sobriety, which is a state of mind freed from obsession or preoccupation with the addiction. We touched on the concepts of abstinence and sobriety in Chapter 1 when I raised the question of what kind of disease might interfere with or disrupt our work together (pages 2-4). I suggested that either by actually engaging in intoxicating behavior, like drinking a fifth of Scotch, or by being preoccupied with the idea of becoming intoxicated, I might be unavailable to attach to you or to our work together. Engaging in intoxicating behavior would represent a break in my abstinence; being preoccupied would remove me from my sobriety.

In psychoanalytic circles, abstinence refers to the analyst's behavior in relation to the analysand, the person being treated. Abstinence is associated with therapeutic neutrality; theoretically the analyst's mind is free of the analyst's own needs, wishes, or demands so as to be able to attend solely to the needs, wishes, and demands of the analysand. Abstinence has also been described as the analyst presenting the analysand with a blank screen onto which the analysand may project feelings and fantasies.

I suggest that in both cases, abstinence for group members and abstinence for group therapist, the group therapist is powerless over abstinence. Some group therapists, both in the field of addictions treatment and in more general practice, make abstinence a prerequisite for joining a group. The problem with setting this kind of exclusionary boundary is that it fosters the illusion of control. If we recognize recovery as a process rather than as an event or as an outcome, then the addict may become abstinent from one part of the addiction, e.g., alcohol, to uncover a seriously disturbed relationship with nicotine, food, sex, money, or another addict. This phenomenon has been described in the general psychotherapy literature as peeling the layers of an onion (sometimes even including an acknowledgment of the accompanying tears).

If we can embrace our powerlessness over the abstinence of those whom we care for, then our work in group therapy and recovery challenges us to join these groups creatively. Our task is to be honest and authentic rather than persuasive or coercive. We do not demand honesty and authenticity from those we serve; we offer opportunities to experience the freedom that accompanies the process of coming out of hiding. If this picture seems idyllic to you, I can assure you that the serenity that accompanies this freedom bears no resemblance to the bucolic tranquility of a sedated or narcotized state. Abstinence and, more pointedly, sobriety bring with them intense emotions such as hurt, anger, fear, sadness, and loneliness. At the risk of hyperbole, I suggest that abstinence and sobriety constitute crises for the addicted group, crises whose impact is analogous to the airliners crashing into the World Trade Center as described in Chapter 1. We will take a closer look at the emergence and metabolism of these emotions in Chapters 6 and 7 respectively.

We may also then be able to welcome our powerlessness over our own abstinence (and sobriety) from the outset of the therapeutic relationship. If we let go of casting ourselves in the role of immovable Buddhalike authorities, and accept a more malleable human posture, then one central task of group therapy becomes an investigation of how we are moved by the group. This movement within the therapist has been called countertransference, and we will also return to this topic in Chapter 6.

The third issue connecting the group therapist's role to powerlessness concerns the agenda for the group therapy sessions. Unfortunately, particularly in the field of addictions treatment, a notion has arisen that the addict will attempt to talk about anything other than the addiction. This phenomenon, assumed to be related to denial, has been called "defocusing," and addictions therapists are trained to confront this defocusing and return the group to its agenda of discussing whatever aspect of addiction or recovery is mandated for that session. The irony of this position becomes apparent if I have accurately portrayed the relationship between powerlessness and free association in Chapter 3 (pages 29-38). According to this portrayal, the addict will inevitably return to thoughts of addiction, whether concretely *or symbolically.* If the group therapist understands and accepts this, then giving the group responsibility for setting the agenda inevitably leads the therapist to an appreciation for how and where the group is struggling for control over its disease. Precisely by practicing powerlessness over the group's agenda, the therapist becomes available to work with the group on its powerlessness. Any predetermined agenda on the therapist's part rescues the group from having to take any ownership in its work. Another way of looking at this issue of agenda setting is that the task of the therapist is to attend to and be mindful of the Higher Power that the group believes in. If the group locates its Higher Power in the group therapist, thus acting in accordance with basic assumption dependence (see page 11), then the therapist's task is to examine with the group the unmanageability of disowning its own role in authorizing the therapist. On the other hand, if the group locates its Higher Power in its addiction, the therapist may applaud the group's honesty and work with the group to examine the parallel difficulties that the group experiences in authorizing its addiction both inside and outside of the treatment. If the therapist becomes critical of the group for its preoccupation with its addiction, then the therapist colludes in the group's adoption of basic assumption fight-flight (see page 11) as the group uses its addiction to engage in a power struggle with the group therapist.

I recognize that I have been offering you a means of understanding the authority of the group therapist that entails dispensing with most of the props that are commonly associated with authority in the mental health arena. Mental health professionals are often indoctrinated in the belief that diagnosis, abstinence, and agenda are events rather than mutually negotiated processes. That the group therapist becomes available to receive a more meaningful authorization by demonstrating powerlessness over the group's diagnosis, abstinence, and agenda is another of the paradoxes involved in recovery from addiction.

Chapter 6

Surrender and Transference

THE DREAM

He dreamed of
an open window.
A vagina, said
his psychiatrist.
Your divorce, said
his mistress.
Suicide, said
an ominous voice within him.
It means you should close the window
or you'll catch cold, said
his mother.
His wife said
Nothing.
He dared not tell her
such a
dangerous dream.

Felix Pollak

What a lovely poem! I feel sad that the poet could not see the window opening to more abundant dreams.

God Almighty, Bea, how much longer can you stay blissed out in this honeymoon state? With all the sex you have, Roth would be well within his rights to interpret the open window as your vagina.

The poet does seem to have his own inner perpetrator. Inner Nigger tells me to blow my brains out on a regular basis.

I don't think I have ever stopped wishing I were dead. And this group is not helping me feel any better. If the window were open here I might jump out myself. I have been thinking about leaving the group.

You can't be serious, Kelly. We have been together in this group for years. I can't imagine what the group would be like without you.

I'm sure the idea terrifies you, Bea. If Kelly left the group you might have to let go of your eternal cheerfulness and pick up some of Kelly's hopelessness.

I suspect that the poem is more autobiographical than Roth wants to admit. I bet his shrink talks to him about vaginas. By the way, Kelly, I support you in leaving group. I see Roth as being as overprotective toward you as the poet's mother is to him.

Suppose we have admitted our powerlessness over the dysfunctional roles we have adopted in our relationships with other people. We have also admitted that the dysfunctional roles have rendered our lives unmanageable. Next we come to believe that we can authorize something outside of ourselves to examine these roles and to engage in a process of recovery. At this point we have the opportunity to make a decision. This decision entails surrendering these dysfunctional roles in all of their gory detail to this power greater than ourselves. In the context of group psychotherapy, surrender means showing the group what the dysfunctional role looks like and feels like. Surrender involves not sparing the group from the experience of relating to someone in the grip of this dysfunctional role.

The first three steps of the Twelve-Step programs have been abbreviated (or simplified) to the following formula: (1) I can't, (2) someone else can, and (3) let them.

If we operationally define a dysfunctional role as the set of behaviors and the set of beliefs about these behaviors that impair the individual's ability to attach to or join a group, then the first step is an acknowledgement that I cannot attach to or join a group while I maintain my dysfunctional role and my belief that this role is an insurmountable obstacle to attachment. I must relax the belief in the omnipotent power of the dysfunctional role and come to believe in a power outside of myself that would support attachment.

You may have an emotional response to the manner in which the members of our group relate to you, to me, and to each other. In particular you may notice that they can be critical, sarcastic, seductive, empathic, and even compassionate. You may experience some of the interactions as inviting attachment and other interactions as distancing. You might even have some judgments about them, finding yourself liking one of them more and finding another of them grating or annoying. On the other hand, you may be totally uninterested in any of them and find yourself doubtful that they contribute anything useful to your understanding of group process. If you are in this role of lacking interest, you might want to return to the exercise at the end of Chapter 3 where we mapped out your position in the group (Chapter 3, page 36). Since we have been joined by Warren and Leslie, if you find yourself unattached to anyone in the group, I suggest that you have positioned yourself as follows (you are still X and the rest of us O):

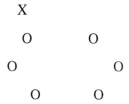

In the context of recovery from addiction and group psychotherapy for recovering addicts, surrender to the process of recovery and therapy may entail discovering that I maintain significant barriers to attachment. If the alcoholic recognizes that impulses to drink will always be available even after years of sobriety, then we as therapists may recognize that impulses to disengage and remain unattached will always be available even after years of practicing as group therapists. Our task then becomes one of using our emotional responses to develop a working relationship with the group. Therefore I challenge you, as reader, to examine your emotional responses to me as author, and to each member of our group. I invite you to look at your impulse

to remain disengaged or unattached, as well as your likes and dis-
likes.

Group therapists may rationalize or justify the suppression of feelings and reactions to the group based on the therapist's position of
power or authority in the group. The motive behind this suppression
relies on an understanding of authority that locates power in the person of the therapist rather than locating this power in the relationship
between therapist and group. This conflict regarding the therapist's
surrender has found expression in psychoanalysis under the rubric of
transference and countertransference.

Why did we drop the poem? I have been imagining seeing the reader through
the open window.

I don't know why you think the reader would care about your
wanting to be noticed. I have been talking about leaving this
damn group, and Dr. Roth does not even seem to hear me.

*Actually, I'm grateful that Leslie brings us back to the poem. I realize
that I have suppressed an association to the poem. It's about the automatic interpretation of the open window as a vagina. That reminds me
of my first psychiatrist, Bob. I saw him because my marriage did not
seem to be working. All Bob seemed interested in was my sex life. He
seemed particularly concerned that I had never had an orgasm.*

None of the psychiatrists I ever saw gave the slightest indication of curiosity about my sex life.

What about Dr. Jansen?

You don 't think that I take that at all seriously? Just because Dr. Roth says that a dozen of Jansen's patients filed
complaints about sexual contact with Dr. Jansen, what could
that possibly have to do with me? Jansen never expressed any
attraction to me.

But you did tell us that Dr. Jansen put you under.

You mean the Amytal interviews?

Yes. Wasn't that the story with his other patients, that he allegedly had sex with them while they were unconscious from the drugs?

But those were attractive patients.

Did we just rescue Bea?

No, we have just heard Bea's story a few more times than you.

Well, I don't know about your Dr. Jansen, Kelly, but Bob was sitting on the couch next to me by our third session. He took my hand and put it on his crotch, and I felt his erection. How strange that it seemed so flattering at the time.

I don't know why you pretend to be so oblivious, Bea. It's not bad enough that you win the competition for Dr. Roth, but you even get to be more attractive to other psychiatrists.

Weren't you terrified, Bea? I remember being comforted by sleeping with my mother, but after she was dead to the world from her sleeping pills she would get up in the middle of the night to use the washroom. Half the time she would come back to bed buck naked. I was excited, scared, and ashamed that I could be turned on by my own mother.

I don't remember being terrified until he started walking his fingers up the inside of my thigh under my skirt and stuck them in my vagina. And yes, Warren, I was also excited, scared, and ashamed that I was being unfaithful to my husband with my psychiatrist who was supposed to be helping me with my marriage.

So how do all these sexually abusive authorities connect to Roth?

You are so busy being a puppet doing Roth's interpretive work for him that he might as well physically put his fist up your butt.

The group's anxiety about sexual contact with me leads to exquisite sensitivity and vigilance.

Herein lies the rub. The group therapist as well as the group finds themselves caught between Scylla and Charybdis. The suction of the whirlpool that pulls the group to repeat self-destructive behavior may be avoided at all costs. Yet steering clear of this whirlpool may drive the group into the cliffs of isolation, as any hint of intimacy becomes a reminder of the wreckage of the past. Warren speaks eloquently of the impact of his family-of-origin's addictions on his adult life. Kelly and Bea offer us examples of how this impact may be expressed through repetition of trauma in a therapeutic relationship. Shall we resign ourselves in hopelessness and despair of ever establishing an intimate connection without descending into a nightmare of abuse?

Let us tackle this issue directly, as we did in the examination of the duration of treatment in Chapter 5 (page 52). Those who are squeamish about the development of dependence on the therapeutic relationship may also have serious misgivings about any boundary crossings between therapist and patient. The most severe critics of any physical contact argue that a "slippery slope" connects the innocent touch of a handshake or a hug to the explicit sexual exploitation described by Bea and Kelly. The critics contend that the only certain method of protecting the patient from abuse is to ban any kind of boundary crossing. Similar arguments have been advanced about therapist self-disclosure and about contact between patient and therapist outside of the office or therapeutic setting. The key assumption here is that if the therapist's behavior is controlled enough, abuse can be prevented. We may notice here the structural similarity between these arguments and the attempts of the addict to control dysfunctional behavior with arbitrary rules. For example, I am not an alcoholic if I drink only after 5:00 p.m. I am not a compulsive overeater if I can skip breakfast and lunch or if I can stay below 200 pounds. I have not had sexual contact with a subordinate if we did not engage in intercourse but had only oral sex.

So perhaps we can do the thought experiment of descending the proverbial slippery slope. Return to Chapter 1 (pages 3-4) where I have polished off a fifth of Scotch. Thanks to Kelly I have been hearing a lot about the benefits of Alcoholics Anonymous, and I can even see her growth as she participates, albeit grudgingly, in a process of recovery. Suppose that I begin to realize that my "social" drinking, which has allowed me to overcome my anxiety about writing this book, has become more of a hindrance than a help. I have actually tried all of the methods that Kelly has shared with me about how to control her drinking by herself. The only avenue that I have not tried is going to AA myself. I even have a marvelous rationalization for not going to AA: What if Kelly were to see me at a meeting? The insanity of my thinking should be clear; I am telling myself that I can help Kelly with her sobriety while I kill myself drinking. I convince myself that I should die of alcoholism rather than risk "harming" Kelly by exposing my addiction to her.

To be fair, some addictions treatment providers who are in recovery themselves have approached this "two-hat" problem by avoiding Twelve-Step meetings if their patients might be present. The fly in the ointment here is the rationalization used for the avoidance. If the therapist is clear that this avoidance serves the purpose of protecting the therapist's privacy, and the therapist is willing to accept the consequences of a more restricted access to the resources of recovery, then the selfishness of this position maintains honesty and integrity in the therapeutic relationship. If, on the other hand, the therapist maintains the belief that attending the same meeting as a patient somehow harms the patient, then the patient becomes implicitly responsible for the barrier to the therapist having full access to recovery.

Imagine, if you will, the alternative. If I need to go to a Twelve-Step meeting, I go. Although I am not responsible for whether someone in treatment with me shows up at the meeting, I do need to be mindful of whether I chose that meeting in order to expose myself to that person. I also need to consider whether I would share information at the meeting for my own benefit or to achieve some impact on that person. Remember the mistake I admitted about my relationship with Kelly in Chapter 5 (page 55)? I suggested that I had jumped into attempting to rescue her. I suspect that one way I attempted to rescue Kelly was by attending a Twelve-Step meeting in order to get her to show up there. Without being aware of the impact of my behavior, I wonder if I was using myself as bait. Ironically, and predictably, neither of us received as much help from the meeting as was available to the extent that I was implicitly there to attract her attendance and that she was there to see me. However, I also suspect that neither of us was impervious to the benefits of hearing the experience, strength, and hope of the others in attendance at the meeting. The limitation on the efficacy of treatment at that time was imposed by my inability to examine this dynamic directly in the therapeutic relationship with Kelly.

Of course, I was also limited by my denial of the scenario from my own life that I was reenacting with Kelly.

That certainly was the time when all the trouble between us started, when you began to bother me with all your talk about reenactments.

These discussions must have taken place before we started in group together because I don't remember them.

But something else is falling into place now. I remember how reluctant you were, Kelly, to talk about seeing Dr. Roth at the meeting. Dr. Roth confronted you on your attempts to protect him, and you steadfastly refused to share anything about it. You claimed that you would be betraying him if you breathed a word about it. The element of betrayal takes me back to my relationship with Bob; I remember how carefully I hid from everyone the sexual relationship that developed in the therapy.

Well, it did not matter a bit to Dr. Roth that I would not share the fact that I saw him at meetings; he still abandoned me by not coming to that meeting anymore.

You can be amazingly exasperating, Kelly! Did it ever occur to you that Dr. Roth might have felt compelled to leave that meeting precisely because your refusal to talk about it made an honest relationship with you impossible?

If the son of a bitch wanted to talk about it, why didn't he bring it up?

Because he is the therapist and it is his job to protect your confidentiality. He went to the limit by confronting you on withholding information about contact with him outside of the group.

Aren't we kissing a little ass, Richard? How do you feel with the shoe on the other foot?

Point well taken, my friend. I'm impressed.

I find this shift in the group significant. As soon as Bea lets go of idealizing me and examines with the group her sexual relationship with her previous psychiatrist, both Richard and Warren are elected by the group to defend my management of the group's boundaries.

When are you going to get a life, Roth? Are you always going to insist that everything we talk about here relates to you?

Leslie's question focuses our attention on the crux of the matter of transference and surrender. One view of psychotherapy holds the therapist as omnipotent authority. The patient asks for help and the therapist dispenses advice, wisdom, or interpretations that fix the patient's problems. The other view, which we have tentatively adopted, holds that the authority resides in the relationship between the therapist and patient(s). According to this view, the only meaningful role for the therapist is to examine the therapeutic relationship and comment on its functionality or impairment. Therefore, for instance, what may appear to be advice or guidance, such as the suggestion to attend a Twelve-Step meeting, may actually function as an indirect interpretation of some way in which the therapeutic relationship might be strengthened. A specific example of such an intervention would be for me to suggest attending an AA meeting to a patient who is trying to control his drinking. If my goal is to stop this patient from drinking, I have abandoned the relationship with the patient in favor of engaging in a struggle with the alcoholism. If I am clear that attending the meeting may actually interfere with the patient's attempt to control the drinking, and in fact may temporarily result in loss of control and increased drinking, then I can honestly tell this person that attending the meeting entails the risk of losing control and also the risk of losing the enjoyment of the drinking. The ultimate purpose, then, of recommending attendance at the AA meeting is to open a conversation about the impact of the attempts to control drinking on the viability of the therapeutic relationship.

So, to answer your question, Leslie, I hope to maintain my commitment to understanding how everything we talk about here relates to us.

Hey, reader, what about you and me splitting from this monotony and having a good time outside of this book?

Actually, in line with my comment about suggesting a Twelve-Step meeting, I support you, Leslie, in inviting the reader to an open Twelve-Step meeting along with the rest of the group.

You have the sneakiest way of turning acting out into something healthy.

Thank you, Leslie.

TWELVE-STEP MEETING

Hi, my name is Leslie, and I am the chair of this meeting.

Hi, Leslie!

Welcome to this open Twelve-Step meeting. Will all who care to, join me in the serenity prayer.

God, grant me the serenity to accept the things I cannot change, courage to change the things I can, and wisdom to know the difference.

Thank you. This meeting lasts for four pages, so please be mindful of the space when making your comments. We also ask that comments reflect the experience of the speaker, and we ask that there be no cross-talk. Finally, what you hear here, when you leave here, let it stay here. The floor is now open for sharing.

Thanks, Leslie. My name is Bea.

Hi, Bea!

Hi, everyone. I am grateful for this meeting. I am at a critical point in my therapy, and my group has been confronting me on my codependence with our therapist. As I have been letting go of taking care of him, I have become more and more enraged at the alcoholic therapist I saw years ago who sexually abused me. My sexual relationship in my new marriage is going better than I could have ever imagined, and I don't want the rage which is coming up to come out indirectly toward my husband. Thanks for the opportunity to share.

Thanks, Bea!

HI. My name is Warren.

Hi, Warren!

Hi, everybody. I just need to turn over my anxiety about a recent promotion at work. I am expecting a lot of pressure to please everyone else to justify the promotion, as if I didn't deserve it. With that, I'll pass.

Thanks, Warren!

Hi. I'm Kelly. I guess I might belong here.

Hi, Kelly. Welcome.

I usually have a difficult time sharing at meetings, which for me are AA meetings. I find myself struggling to say something interesting or entertaining. I have always told myself that I am too socially awkward to fit in anywhere. I pass.

You are in the right place.

Thanks, Kelly.

I'll take a turn now. Thanks for all of your comments so far. Oh, and I am still Leslie, recovering codependent.

Hi, Leslie!

Hi, everybody. Well I am still wondering whether I am being a people pleaser in chairing this meeting. The idea kind of arose from my therapist, who suggested I invite someone to a meeting instead of trying to control the relationship by being seductive. I am not sure what the result is supposed to be, but I'll keep coming back and see what happens.

Thanks, Leslie.

I would like to add that if anyone here prefers not to share, you may simply introduce yourself and say "I pass."

Hi. My name is Richard.

Hi, Richard.

Thanks for your comment, Leslie. I identify with the question of why I am at this meeting. I am aware that much of what I do seems motivated by the desire to please other people, and I am struggling with how much of my being here is for me and how much is for everyone else.

Thanks, Richard.

Hi. I'm the reader.

Hi, reader.

I pass.

Thanks, reader. Keep coming back!

We have come to the end of our meeting. Will all who care to, join me in closing with the prayer **"I put my hand in yours and together we can do what we could never do alone. No longer is there a sense of hopelessness. No longer must we each depend upon our own unsteady willpower. We are all together now reaching out our hands for a power and strength greater than our own. And, as we join hands we find love and understanding beyond our wildest dreams."***

* * *

One pitfall of individual psychotherapy is that the patient can more easily maintain the illusion of uniqueness. In contrast to group psychotherapy, in which multiple relationships are being transacted at all times, individual therapy creates a relationship that cannot be immediately compared to other relationships in a moment-to-moment analysis. Now one can certainly conduct a therapy group in a manner where these multiple relationships are obscured or rendered unspeakable. For example, a therapist who adopts a caricature of the Tavistock consultant's stance may avoid any interaction with individual members of a therapy group. The justification for this stance is usually that the therapist is focusing on the group as a whole. Ironically, the problem with this stance can be most easily understood using the wisdom garnered from group-as-a-whole theorists. If the group is using one of its members to express some wish or feeling in its relationship with the therapist, then the therapist may have to be willing to engage with this member in order to learn about what this member is carrying and how this member is being used by the group. Thus the primary difference between doing individual therapy in a group versus viewing the entire group as the object of therapy has mostly to do with what is in the therapist's mind. I aspire to be able to

---

*Al-Anon closing, 1964, reprinted by permission of Al-Anon Family Group Headquarters, Inc.

listen to the individual without losing sight of the fact that I am really listening to a representative of the group.

Therefore I suggest it is inevitable in a therapy group that the therapist develops special differentiated relationships with each member of the group. This differentiation places us squarely on that slippery slope I referred to earlier in relation to boundary crossings. One way boundary crossings have been recognized in psychotherapy is in the creation of dual relationships. So returning to Bea's experience with her psychiatrist, Bob, a dual relationship of doctor-patient and lovers was established. However, I suggest that the therapeutic relationship is always a dual relationship: doctor to patient and human being to human being. Perhaps the important issue in group psychotherapy is not how to prevent special relationships, but how to understand them and work with them so that the human-to-human relationship is mutually beneficial rather than toxic and destructive. Because group members ideally have an opportunity to experience, observe, and talk about the special relationships that develop in a group, these relationships may actually be supported and evolve in more functional directions. I hope that I supported such an evolution, for example, in suggesting that Leslie conduct a meeting that you, the reader, might attend. I also want to alert you that my own absence from this meeting is intentional. I am aware of the likelihood that, because of your relative silence in the role of reader, the group, through Leslie, may attempt to transact part of its relationship with me through you. I also want to be explicit about the special relationship that exists between you as reader and me as author. While we are together, and the group witnesses the way I talk to you, the group may have difficulty negotiating a more direct relationship with you. I hope that my absence from the meeting offered an opportunity for you to see the difference in how people may work in therapy groups and Twelve-Step groups, and also for you to develop a more independent relationship with the members of the group. The additional implications of this kind of contact among members outside of group provide expanded opportunities for members of the group to create personal inventories through reenactments, which we will examine in Chapter 7.

Chapter 7

Inventory and Reenactment

I want to talk about the reader coming to a meeting with us.

So are you happy now, Leslie? You think you have the reader wrapped around your finger?

That's not what I see at all, Kelly. Leslie seemed a lot less seductive at the meeting than when we first met the reader here. Maybe you need Leslie to stay in that role.

What the hell are you talking about, Richard?

I'm not sure myself. But you do seem pretty angry. Maybe you are pissed off at Leslie for violating the no cross-talk guideline at our meeting. I know that I noticed Leslie commenting on what you were saying.

Were you angry, Richard?

More of a mixture of fear and joy that I was seeing a side of Leslie that is not usually available in group.

Thanks, Richard. Anyway, having the reader come with us led me to realize that we have been maintaining some distance from the reader by withholding our stories.

I was also thinking along those lines. Even though I am not ordinarily big on storytelling, we do have a lot of history with one another that the reader does not share. If we treated any other new group member the way we have treated the reader, I would have to conclude that we were colluding in shunning the reader.

When I did share the part of my story about my daddy's drinking and my mom sleeping with me, I felt intense shame. IN was kicking my ass about airing dirty laundry in front of yet another person who would not understand and

would not care. IN told me that the reader was already forming judgments about how another worthless nigger was trying to buy his freedom by throwing his family to the wolves.

Well just in case you idiots think you can please Dr. Roth by telling your stories, let me tell you that I already tried that in Chapter 1, and all I got for my troubles was a reprimand from Dr. Roth about how I was being distant.

Hold on there, Kelly. Did you just admit that you told your story to please Dr. Roth?

Of course, Richard. I would do anything to get his attention.

So can you imagine that trying to get Dr. Roth's attention might interfere with your having honest relationships with us and being a full-fledged member of this group?

You seem to forget that I have had serious reservations about joining this group in the first place, and I have also talked about leaving.

You know, Kelly, we have both talked about being abused by psychiatrists in our adult life.

I never said that I was abused by a psychiatrist.

Sorry. You have talked about treatment that the rest of us have questions about. But you have also told us about experiences with a doctor you had as a child.

You mean my mother's doctor?

Yeah.

I don't know what this has to do with anything, or why the reader would be interested. But my mother was always sure that someone in our family would develop cancer. When I was young she was obsessed with the idea that I would die of leukemia. I had similar ruminations about my own children. Anyway, she was sure she had breast cancer, and she would visit her cousin Arthur who was a homeopath. I would have to go with her on these visits at his office every Saturday, and I would sit in an adjacent room with the door open while Arthur would massage her breasts. Mother would make these pained appreciative noises, and I would feel embarrassed by her tone, which was otherwise ordinarily harsh and critical.

It sounds like she was having an orgasm.

I wouldn't know.

That's right. You did say at some point you had never had an orgasm.

Why are you so intent on humiliating me?

The presence of the reader here as witness seems to highlight the group's shame.

I can identify with Kelly's experience of humiliation. Two memories come to the surface. My mother's brother is a chiropractor, and I used to spend some time with his sons, my cousins. I was about five years old and they were a few years older. We were in their backyard playing tetherball. The ground around the pole was muddy. I slipped and fell with my face in the mud, and my cousins laughed hysterically. I started crying, and they got mad at me. They threatened to give me something to cry about if I did not stop. I got scared and cried even more loudly. They pulled my pants down and while one of them pushed my face in the mud the other put his finger up my ass. When they finally let me up I ran into their kitchen to my mother. I tried to tell her what had happened through my tears, but she shushed me, took me to the bathtub, and told me everything was fine.

No wonder you were so sensitive about the idea that Roth has his hand up my butt.

Actually, it's worse. And right now, I am telling myself that you all have a hard enough time believing the story I just told. You will never believe the other part of the story.

You think we have as much difficulty hearing you as your mother did?

I guess. Just be honest with me if you don't believe what I am about to say. When I hit puberty, I got these violent headaches. Mom took me to see my uncle, the chiropractor. He told us that the treatment for migraine was a spinal adjustment at the level of the coccyx. So for several months we would visit him, and he would stick his finger up my ass to do this manipulation of my tailbone.

Jesus, Leslie, if your uncle had his finger up your ass, what makes you think that he spared his sons that kind of abuse?

And maybe that's connected with your cousins doing the same thing to you!

Oh my God. I'm expecting you not to believe me, and you manage to connect these two stories in a way I had never imagined.

Well, I must admit it is a lot easier for me to see in you what I still have some denial about for myself. Before I came to treatment with Dr. Roth, I not only blamed myself for seducing Bob, but I also thought that my mother's routine administration of enemas through my adolescence was a normal all-American tradition.

Did you ever think that the abuse by Bob could be connected to being buttfucked by your mother?

Again, Leslie, you can probably see that more easily than I can.

So what exactly are we doing here? Are we setting up the reader to be filled up with our toxic experiences? Is Roth using us to stick us up the reader's butt? Or has Roth invited the reader to witness his abuse of us?

Richard, do you think you could step off your interpretive soapbox for a few minutes to just join us?

Thanks for confronting me, Leslie. Though I still think the questions I raise are legitimate. But I understand that all of this talk about getting buttfucked might be a trigger for me. I first came to see Roth after becoming acutely anxious; maybe I had my first panic attack. It happened at the tail end, so to speak of a sexual relationship that was becoming increasingly bizarre. My lover was insisting, demanding actually, that we engage in fisting. While I was not enthusiastic about that being done to me, oddly enough what really terrified me was fisting someone else. I still don't know what all was stirred up in me by that episode.

Although I appreciate that some of the stories you are hearing from group members may be shocking or disturbing, I hope you recognize the significance of the group's willingness to share these stories with you. Now you may protest that the stories on these pages are written in this book whether you read it or not. I would then point out that the authorization for these stories to be transmitted to you is mutual; group members must be willing to share and you must be willing to read and witness. Both the group and you have had to surrender to our work together for the Twelve-Step meeting to take place in Chapter 6 and for the group to delve into its inventory in this chapter.

Inventory work, encompassing steps four and five of the Twelve-Step programs, entails learning about who we are and sharing this learning with at least one other person, with our Higher Power, and with ourselves. We learn about our past and about how we relate in the present, including all of the feelings that we have suppressed or distorted through denial, justification, and rationalization. We began an examination of reenactments in Chapter 4 (page 42). If we accept that the reenactment is a concrete link between the past and how we relate to others in the present, then the examination of reenactments in the group becomes the royal road to the group's inventory (parts of the group mind that the group might prefer to remain unaware of). To extend this metaphor, analysis of reenactments may be as fruitful in group therapy as dream analysis is in individual therapy.

I cannot emphasize enough the centrality of feelings in this inventory work that is transacted in groups through reenactments. The intellectual memories that connect the past and the present do not account for the intensity with which the reenactment is experienced and held onto. One classical form of inventory taking in Twelve-Step programs involves making a list of resentments concerning the people and situations in our lives that we have maintained resentments toward. Resentments can be understood as feelings that have been suppressed or withheld. These feelings are invariably justified. In fact, the ubiquity of justified feelings is such that many people cannot imagine having feelings that are not justified.

Consider as an example the interaction between Richard and Kelly in this chapter (page 75) in which Richard remembers that Kelly has said that she never had an orgasm. Kelly might feel shame about this limitation in her sexuality, but instead of recognizing and owning her shame, she automatically justifies her shame by accusing Richard of humiliating her. Now we might speculate that, in witnessing her mother having her breasts fondled by a family member, Kelly was used by her mother to contain shame for the family, particularly if Richard was accurate in his association that the function of the massage was sexual excitement rather than therapy.

The crucial dynamic here is that in justifying the feeling, the person is blaming someone or something else for the feeling. The feeling itself is disavowed as if it did not belong to the justifier. Imagine the difficulty Kelly might have experiencing her sexual feelings if she blamed someone else for these feelings rather than owning them herself. Suppose that the shame about sexuality overwhelmed any ability to enjoy a sexual experience.

Stop picking on me!

I'm sorry, Kelly. I believe that I have relapsed into offering help that has not been asked for.

Alternatively, consider this dynamic in an alcoholic family. Let's say Mom is drinking. Perhaps she feels hurt and lonely in not having a more intimate relationship with Dad. Dad may be working hard, even working compulsively. Perhaps he is late for dinner. Mom, who is trying to maintain the illusion of control over her drinking, has promised herself not to start drinking before dinner. But now the undependable husband has come home late once again, and Mom is justified in her resentment. Besides, the kids are complaining about dinner being late, so Mom starts dinner without Dad. As long as dinner is served, Mom can now justifiably start drinking.

Hey, Roth. Are you now telling my story to the reader to get back at me for exposing Kelly?

As Warren points out, the telling of the story with feelings attached may be experienced as a betrayal of the family. If we take seriously the depth of commitment on the family's part to maintaining secrecy in order to preserve the addiction, then in fact a family member sharing the secrets does constitute a betrayal of the addiction. The primary betrayal may involve violation of two central rules in addiction: do not feel feelings and do not share feelings. Making a list of resentments, then, is also a violation of these rules of addiction. The act of listing the resentments without medicating them with the addiction results in a surge of feelings. Step Five involves sharing the inventory and all of the attendant feelings with God, oneself, and another human being. The act of admitting the resentments to oneself and someone else with the awareness of authorizing a Higher Power to hear these feelings results in a transmission of feelings that constitutes the foundation of intimate attachment.

Let us return to the beginning of this chapter. Leslie wanted to talk about the experience of your going to the Twelve-Step meeting with the group. I suggest that to the extent the group has been sharing its inventory work that you have functioned in the role of another human being as indicated in Step Five. If I am accurate in my portrayal of Step Five as necessarily involving the transmission of feelings, then I would anticipate that you as reader, witness, and another human being might have had some feelings associated with the group's examination of painful experiences from the past. Whether your feelings involved shock, horror, excitement, disgust, terror, or grief is less critical than that something was transmitted. So I ask you at this point to pause and consider what feelings, if any, surfaced in you. If you choose to examine these feelings or reflect on what may have inhibited an emotional response in you, then you are also participating in the group's inventory as a mutual process.

Notice also that in your role as reader you do not have the opportunity to comment directly on anything you hear from other members of the group, even though they are free to comment about you. Richard confronted Leslie on violating the no cross-talk guideline at the Twelve-Step meeting when Leslie commented on Kelly's sharing. Because of the silence implicit in your role, you are the one member of the group who inevitably surrenders to this guideline of no cross-talk. The structure of the Twelve-Step meeting with no cross-talk creates an opportunity for all group members to identify with the speaker and for feelings to move from speaker to listeners. We might name this movement of feelings "e-motion" to emphasize the role of feelings in establishing an attachment. E-motion is accomplished in group psychotherapy through reenactment, wherein the whole group participates in experiencing feelings and sharing feelings.

For those of us who grew up in families with addictions, feelings were burdens to be medicated. The so-called positive feelings of joy or gratitude necessitated a drink or festive meal to temper their passion. The negative feelings of sadness, anger, hurt, and loneliness were avoided and suppressed using a versatile combination of compulsive behaviors and enabling. The only feeling that was ubiquitous was shame, but because this shame was never shared openly, even this feeling could not be used as a means for members of the family to attach. Indeed, in the context of the family suffering from an addiction, the very notion of using any feeling as a means to attach is counterintuitive.

Consider what may happen when intensely painful feelings are openly shared rather than suppressed or medicated. Let us take as an example Leslie's descriptions of abuse with the cousins and with the uncle. Especially given Leslie's expectations that these stories are not believable, I suggest that we explicitly agree not to become sidetracked into an argument about whether these memories are historically accurate. Suffice it to say that these memories may function to justify a certain distance that Leslie maintains from the group. Parenthetically, these memories may also function to justify Leslie's compulsion to pull you in, hoping against hope that you will be the first person not to frustrate, disappoint, or violate her in the manner prescribed by these memories. Now when Warren and Bea openly demonstrate their compassion for Leslie in understanding these memories and connecting the memories to one another, the members of the group become more connected to one another. Richard, for whom all connections need to be examined with an attitude of skepticism, then wonders aloud how these revelations may relate to the group's relationship with you.

Before we leave the issue of historical accuracy, I would also suggest that the accuracy of Warren's and Bea's hypotheses about Leslie's uncle abusing his children is also not necessary to the process of the group's attachment. If the hypothesis is based on some group distortion, then the important issue is whether the group can work on understanding this distortion in its relationship with me. Richard's role in maintaining the group's capacity to raise these questions about my authority helps to create balance and safety. To the extent that memories of intrusion from the past can emerge as conflicts about intrusion in the present, we can dispense with historical accuracy in favor of an honest and accurate picture of the here and now, and this accuracy can only be constructed interdependently using the perspectives of each member of the group.

Ironically, as we let go of old dysfunctional roles and the maladaptive ways of medicating feelings that went with those roles, we begin to see the patterns we learned in our families much more clearly. Even if we are fortunate enough to have had our family of origin engaged in a process of recovery, the patterns of addiction do not disappear; they only become more openly speakable (see Chapter 10). Historical accuracy gives way to a mutual appreciation for the patterns of addiction that we do not have to struggle to remember because they are plainly visible in the present.

Another aspect of the process of sharing feelings deserves our attention. Some families with addictions maintain the illusion of being open with their feelings by using feelings as weapons. The most explicit form of this pattern is in the construct "You made me angry," "You hurt me," or "You are scaring me." These statements accomplish three ends. First, the one who wields the emotional weapons gets to blame someone else for his or her own feelings. I deny that I feel angry, hurt, or afraid by making you responsible for my feelings. I also manage to implicitly or explicitly justify my anger, hurt, or fear on the basis of your behavior. Finally, because you are to blame for my "negative" feelings, you are supposed to feel shame about your behavior, which leaves me free to further medicate my feelings with my addictive behavior and leave you holding onto shame for both of us.

You seem to have forgotten about us again.

This time I agree with you, Kelly. I feel hurt that Roth did not respond to my confronting him about telling my story to the reader without my permission.

I feel guilty about enjoying your pain, but I must admit that I feel less lonely with you joining me in being ignored by Dr. Roth.

Well, I think Roth must really be losing it, because he has also broken a promise he made to the reader in Chapter 1. He made an obscure point about metabolizing conflict through expressing feelings with the result of exporting toxicity. He said he would explain it in this chapter.

You are hopelessly loyal, Richard. Even when you experience Roth ignoring and betraying you, you still carry out his agenda as if you were his fucking Palm Pilot beeping him to remind him that he made a commitment.

But isn't that what Dr. Roth has been working with us to understand? That we each play a role in supporting one another. I admit that I also feel afraid that Dr. Roth may need us, given my experience with my mother.

Odd that you put it that way, Warren. I just remembered that when I was a young boy, my father would often lie down in bed with me. It seemed comforting to me at the time, but it never occurred to me that he might have been seeking comfort from me that he could not get from my distant, intoxicated mother.

So now I am curious, Richard. What about this idea of exporting toxicity?

I don't know about you, Leslie, but for me what was toxic as a child was both having to be responsible for my parents and not being able to talk with them about this experience. I appreciate your confronting me about my taking care of Roth largely because you support me in being able to talk about that experience here. I am also learning that I can talk about this caretaking at Twelve-Step meetings, and your presence there is also somehow comforting to me even if I do get confused about our different roles at the meeting and in this group. Actually, I need to admit that the disruption of our usual roles at the Twelve-Step meeting was actually helpful in allowing me to see the role that I play here.

I have a silly idea. I am embarrassed to tell you. But I remember when my youngest daughter, Jody, was a baby she had serious colic. I would become anxious, as if I had caused Jody's pain. Thank God I had some help taking care of the kids, because the woman who was helping me showed me how to gently pat Jody on her back. After a few minutes Jody would either burp or fart, sometimes both.

You're funny, Bea. You think that is what Roth means by exporting toxicity?

I hadn't thought about it this way with my feelings, but this is how it works in my conversations with IN. The more I try to defend myself from IN's insinua-

tions, the more stuck I get. And I know I'm in real trouble when I start to blame other people for the crazy messages I hear from IN. The only thing that seems to help me is to admit to someone, anyone, exactly what IN is saying to me. That's what hit me when I saw that movie, <u>A Beautiful Mind.</u> How he talks to these people and takes them so seriously at first until he recognizes that they are constructed by his own mind. They don't disappear after that; they don't ever go away. Like I don't really ever expect IN to disappear. Just my relationship with IN may change.

Sometimes I feel ashamed about how long I have been in treatment with Roth. I wonder whether I would have been finished a long time ago if he had pushed me to dump my shit sooner.

In order to do that, he would have had to administer an emotional enema.

I guess I'm okay with Roth gently patting me on the back.

You seemed pretty pissed off when you thought he pushed you a little while ago.

I guess I want to be pushed and have the right to feel angry about it at the same time.

I want to thank the group for helping me to honor my commitments. I suspect that one benefit of having gone to the Twelve-Step meeting together is that the group can work with me without being paralyzed by the idea that all of the help comes from me. I also benefit from the group's progress in being able to support the group by being more of a witness myself. Perhaps with the reader assuming a more active role in attending the Twelve-Step meeting, I have been given the space to observe more.

Chapter 8

Humility and Working Through

The natural consequences of letting go of isolation in order to become attached to a group include experiencing a loss of control over relationships and learning how to find a place in these relationships that involves mutual dependence. Whether the group is a psychotherapy group, a Twelve-Step group or this group in this book, the opportunity to practice being one human being among others, neither higher nor lower, neither worthier nor more despicable, becomes available to the extent that the group as a whole is carrying a message of recovery. Precisely this sense of equality provides the core of humility.

Now this equality does not imply a lack of differentiation. One of the challenges of recovery is the recognition that different does not mean better or worse, higher or lower. Although exceptions are inevitable, Twelve-Step groups are among the most accepting and welcoming intentional communities to be found. For the group in recovery, "acceptance is the key." Acceptance of one's own addiction and acceptance of all of the character defects that are associated with the addiction makes one available to have these defects removed by one's Higher Power. As we find out exactly who we are, and as we share ourselves without reservation with others, we practice an acceptance of ourselves and others.

This acceptance has two practical implications for group psychotherapy with recovering addicts. First, while we may share many common features of recovery, such as using the Twelve Steps, each recovering person has a special path. One aspect of this path relates to how the person uses the Twelve Steps. At one extreme, some people in recovery hit bottom with one particular form of addiction, say alcohol. These people may work the Twelve Steps with reference to their alcohol use while maintaining an active addiction such as nicotine, food, sex, money, or codependence. Because they are clearly engaged in another addiction, other people, both in and out of recovery, may depreciate their recovery. Acceptance would guide us to respect the willingness of these alcoholics to clear up a segment of their lives, trusting that the process of surrendering their alcoholism would ultimately lead to surrendering other addictions. At the opposite end of the spectrum are addicts who need to hit bottom with all of their addictions in order to truly embrace their powerlessness. Their path in recovery may look much slower because the changes in their lives are spread out over a larger area of addictions. Perhaps an analogy would be useful. Imagine a rough-hewn wooden floor covering your living room. In order to avoid splinters in your feet, you cover the floor with carpeting. If you want to have a smooth well-polished wooden surface, you might employ two different strategies. You could remove a small section of the carpet and begin sanding the wooden floor with a coarse abrasive and, in step-wise fashion, proceed to use finer and finer abrasives on this small section. You could then gradually, at your leisure, work on each area of the living room floor until the job was complete. The advantage of this method is that you maintain your living room space in its entirety by compromising on having both wood and carpet under your feet. The alternative strategy is to remove all of the carpeting at once and sand the whole floor with the same sequence of coarse and finer abrasives. The advantage of this method is that you get to do the whole job in one pass through the steps.

In practice, I suggest that no one in recovery falls into either extreme of working on only one area of powerlessness at a time or working on every last aspect of powerlessness at one time. In spite of the remarkable acceptance of differences within the culture of recovery, some conflict occasionally emerges between followers of these two approaches to recovery. Those who focus on one area of recovery at a time may portray those who are involved in multiple areas of recovery (and frequently attend multiple kinds of Twelve-Step meetings) as dabblers or dilettantes who are lacking in commitment. Relapses among those pursuing multiple areas of recovery may be viewed as indications of failure to recover. Those who see themselves as multiply addicted may portray their more single-minded brethren in recovery as fanatical "step-Nazis."

Speaking of step-Nazis, I have been wondering about starting on medication.

What does medication have to do with step-Nazis?

If I understand correctly, many old-timers in AA have been very wary of medication.

They act as if all medication were like Valium. They call it "solid alcohol."

I have been open at my meetings about being on medication, and no one has ever criticized me about it.

Can you really be admitting to us that you have ever had the experience of being accepted?

Thanks for reminding me, Leslie. I need to ask Dr. Roth to renew my prescription.

What do you need?

Can't you for once just give me a refill without going through all this rigmarole?

Come on, Bea, you know the drill. First, Roth is not going to relieve you of responsibility for making a direct request for what you want . . .

And second, Dr. Roth would not collude with us by withholding the information about your medication from the reader.

And third, the sly bastard is using us to demonstrate to the reader how medication can be handled in group therapy with recovering addicts.

Ten points and a gold star for you, Richard.

Well, I am angry about having to play this game!

There you go again, Bea, proving Roth's point. What did he tell you when you first started on the medication?

Richard, please. As if I weren't humiliated enough having to ask for a goddamned refill every time.

Unfortunately, Bea, I can see Richard's point. You dig yourself in deeper with every justification.

Okay, you guys, I surrender. Dr. Roth suggested that medication was a complicated issue for us given my history with Bob. Bob had given me Thorazine when I first started seeing him. I got pretty spacey and drugged up on that medication. Maybe that contributed to my being vulnerable to his sexual advances.

Oh boy! Another reenactment. Bob gets you to perform for him sexually by giving you meds, and Roth gets you to perform in this book by giving you meds.

Well, Richard, I guess it's my turn to defend Dr. Roth. At least now Bea gets to be open with her shame about the sexual abuse and about needing medication. And the medication she takes does seem to help her express her anger, even at her idol, Dr. Roth.

So when all this discussion is finished, I still want my drugs. Prozac, ten milligrams a day for a month.

Thank you. Here is your prescription.

Actually, Bea, as much as I hate to admit this, you are helping me to understand some of the feelings I have had in therapy with Dr. Roth. When I first came to see him, I was loaded up on ten milligrams of Xanax a day. Before I got sober I would take that much Xanax, which my friends in AA tell me equals a fifth or two of vodka a day, and then I would drink a fifth of vodka on top of that. Dr. Roth gradually reduced my Xanax until I had totally withdrawn from it over six months. But I was not aware of any shame or anger until I told myself he had withdrawn his love from me.

I can certainly identify with mistaking my substances of abuse with love.

Don't push me too far with your identification.

Because secrecy and isolation are the major lynchpins sustaining the disease of addiction, sharing the exact nature of the addiction, including all of the feelings attached to it, with other people is a crushing blow to maintaining the addiction. Repeatedly breaking the code of silence, asking for help, and being emotionally vulnerable result in the addict becoming entirely ready for a power greater than the addict to remove the defects of character that maintain the disease. The different ways that medication can be used in the treatment of addiction illustrate the contrast between maintaining the illusion of control versus supporting recovery.

I propose here a mechanism of action for medication that includes the pharmacological, emotional, psychological, and spiritual dimensions of the process of prescribing medication. The underlying difference between maintaining the illusion of control versus supporting recovery emerges in whether the doctor-patient system is embracing its powerlessness over feelings. Let us draw from our experience with a common drug, alcohol, which has a familiar dose response curve. I ingest a small amount of alcohol and the major psychopharmacological effect is that I am disinhibited. What we mean by this in emotional terms is that I feel less shame and that I may express other feelings that I would otherwise normally suppress like anger, sadness, or hurt. If I am disrupted by the emergence of these other feelings, I may drink more to feel less. Depending on my tolerance for alcohol, I may drink enough to suppress all emotions, becoming sleepy, dissociated, or unconscious. We may infer from our experience with alcohol that the mechanism for suppressing shame may be more sensitive than the mechanism for suppressing other feelings.

Compare the process of alcohol intoxication with the prescribed use of antidepressants. First note that many of the central symptoms of depression correspond to messages that convey shame. We do not have to stretch to see that the feelings of guilt, unworthiness, and self-blame, which are ubiquitous in depression, depend on shame for their toxicity. We may need to expand our thinking slightly to observe that suicidal ideation translates into the shaming message "I do not deserve to live." Now the receptor pharmacology of alcohol and antidepressants are clearly different. Most important for our purposes, no convincing data exist to support the idea that antidepressants generate unmanageability over which the sufferer is powerless. However, if shame is selectively inhibited at lower doses of antidepressants than required to inhibit anger, sadness, and hurt, some important clinical implications emerge.

If we examine the interpersonal process between a doctor and a patient who are both maintaining the illusion of control, we can immediately dispense with the straw man example of the doctor who explicitly functions as a drug pusher. The physician who responds to the anxiety or insomnia of the patient with an endless supply of anxiolytics without asking about the source of the anxiety and without asking about the patient's use of alcohol or other mood-altering processes is a well-known enabler among recovering addicts. Similarly, the physician may prescribe narcotics to relieve pain without being sensitive to the painful emotional states that the patient may also be medicating.

At the next level of complexity are ways in which doctor and patient implicitly engage in a power struggle with the patient's addiction. This dynamic is well illustrated by the use of stimulants like amphetamine in the treatment of obesity. By naming the problem obesity, doctor and patient focus on the patient's weight as the enemy. The day-to-day process of the patient's attempt to control food intake is ignored. In particular, no attention can be given to the feelings that the patient medicates by overeating, restricting, or purging. So for the patient who is stuck in powerlessness about overeating, the physician may support the patient in restricting by prescribing a stimulant medication that counters the sedating effect of excess food. The physician attempting to treat the drinking alcoholic for depression creates the same dynamic. Let us for a moment let go of the chicken versus egg debate over which came first, the alcoholism or the depression. Suffice to say that in adequate doses alcohol functions as a depressant. Now if the physician prescribes an antidepressant for the drinking alcoholic, the patient may experience some therapeutic benefit. The fly in the ointment is that the therapeutic benefit may appear as the emergence of suppressed feelings such as anger, hurt, sadness, or fear. The patient who is still drinking invariably has little or no willingness or support to feel these feelings. The path of least resistance when challenged by these feelings is to drink more. The physician may then struggle with the patient either explicitly by attempting to control the drinking or implicitly by battling the alcoholism with the antidepressants. An analogous strategy accounts for the use of Antabuse with nonrecovering alcoholics, with the additional dynamic that the alcoholic is threatened with punishment for being powerless over alcohol.

Returning to Bea's request for medication, we can now look at a common source of missed cooperation between the recovering community and the professional community. Unfortunately, many of us suffer from the misconception that once the addict stops using a drug or process, life becomes rosy and cheerful. Actually, enough recovering addicts experience a window of bliss early in recovery to give the name "pink cloud" abstinence to this condition. Frequently though, as the addict reintegrates into the world outside, other feelings challenge this pink cloud. Particularly as the recovering addict faces the active addiction in the family of origin, the current family, the workplace, and friends, continued sobriety depends critically on the recovering addict's ability to feel anger, sadness, hurt, loneliness, and fear and to use these feelings as signals to attach to the culture of recovery. Even the well-intentioned physician is susceptible to interpreting these "negative" feelings as further symptoms of depression. The knee-jerk response is to increase the dosage of antidepressant until the patient's capacity to feel anger, hurt, sadness, fear, and loneliness is impaired. An alternative strategy is provided by the culture of recovery, where those new in recovery are warned to pay close attention to these feelings using the acronym HALT (for *h*ungry, *a*ngry, *l*onely, and *t*ired). These signals are indications that the addict needs to stop or halt whatever else is happening and attend a meeting, call a sponsor, or take whatever action results in attaching to the support of recovery.

When the recovering addict does become depressed, often about a year into the recovery process, the depression is an indication that painful feelings are not available for use in attaching. Failure to attach to others in recovery at this point is a common trigger for relapse. At this point if the recovering addict has established sufficient support to use painful feelings to attach, the use of an antidepressant at a dose that interferes with shame but not other feelings may be therapeutic. Additional complications occur when attachment is attempted using sex as a substitute for emotional intimacy or when attachment is avoided because even neutralized sexuality is ruthlessly suppressed.

Speaking of suppressing sexuality, the Prozac you gave me did a number on my sex drive.

Apparently not enough of a number. Since you became involved with Russ, you have been fucking like a bunny.

I have also been puzzled about that, Leslie. After spending ten years with no sexual contact at all, I thought I was doomed to celibacy. I had gone from being a passive receptacle for my first husband's daily ritual emissions to a period of terrifying promiscuous one-night stands, to a long-term uncommitted nonrelationship. That's when I started seeing Dr. Roth. I suppose when keeping Dr. Roth at a distance didn't work, I fell in love with him.

At least he had the decency to return your love.

Would you really allow anyone to love you, Kelly?

How can you ask me that, Leslie? When I thought that Dr. Roth loved me, I was the happiest I had ever been in my whole life.

Did you have any sexual feelings about him?

I can remember times during sessions when I would feel warm and become moist down there.

Did you ever mention that to Roth?

Of course not. I can't believe that I am talking about it now. When it was happening, I was way too embarrassed to talk about it.

So what did you do with all those sexual feelings? Did you masturbate?

Leslie! There you go again. Asking me these humiliating questions. Don't you know that I have never been able to masturbate?

You haven't explored your vagina or your clitoris?

Why would I? I never enjoyed sex. Most of the time my ex-husband wanted to go to bed I prepared myself with some stiff drinks, a few tranquilizers, and some cigarettes before and after the unpleasant exercise.

Maybe because sex is so important to me I feel sorry for how cut off you are from your sexuality.

Don't patronize me, you condescending bitch!

You know what, Kelly? You can't keep us at a distance anymore with your victimized hostility.

We'll see.

I have an idea that might help both of us, Kelly.

What now?

Well, I have been realizing about myself that I locate all of my power in my sexuality. And you seem to disengage your sexuality as much as possible.

So?

I was wondering what would happen to our roles in this group if you were to make your clitoris into your Higher Power.

What would my poor momma be saying about me spending up my money listening to crazy white folk talking about praying to pussy?

Interesting question, Warren. But hasn't that been a major part of your problem? Seems like you were just complaining about feeling afraid of getting pussy-whipped by your new boss.

Touché, Richard.

I have to admit that despite all of my years in AA, I have never quite understood what it means to have a Higher Power.

Sure you did. Except you seem to have identified your Higher Power as Roth's penis. I actually like Leslie's idea.

As much as I find my genitals disgusting, I do trust you a little, Richard. But you find Leslie's idea crazy, don't you, Warren?

I think my initial response came from IN. I've got to agree with Richard about my worshipping pussy. It's consistent with my sleeping with my mother. So you might be doing me a favor, too.

Since power comes from dicks, Kelly, you can disregard me and listen to Richard and Warren.

Good point, Bea. But give Kelly a break. She might be detoxing off of Roth's dick and making her way to finding some joy in her clitoris.

So, Kelly. Do we have a deal?

Strangely enough, Leslie, I need to ask one more question, and I'm not sure I can get an answer to this one. What does the reader think about your idea?

Are you willing to take on my interest in the reader as well?

I celebrate with the group its willingness to have its failure to attach removed. I also congratulate your ingenuity in devising a solution to the stalemate of using sexual energy as a barrier for everyone in the group. Now, if only the group can locate all of its judgments about the solution in the reader, we can pretend that the problem is resolved.

I thought the idea of me making my clitoris my Higher Power was confusing, but I don't know what the hell you're talking about.

I think Roth is suggesting that we hope the reader doesn't like the idea of you deifying your clitoris. It's such a disruptive suggestion that we need someone to disapprove of it.

Kind of like asking the reader to be IN for the group.

Wow! Exactly.

Since we're talking about the reader, I realize that I have had the fantasy that the reader is a devout religious person. I guess I have not considered the possibility that Inner Nigger might also be very religious. It came to mind when I thought the reader would find the idea of Kelly praying to her clitoris heretical, profane, and blasphemous.

Actually I see the reader as a more scientific type. Though interestingly, I have imagined the reader looking askance at Leslie's idea, but for different reasons. I thought the reader might have had a difficult time buying all of

Roth's crap about authority in Chapter 5. After all, God and prayer have hardly been discussed as scientific topics. So suggesting that Kelly adopt her clitoris as her Higher Power should push the reader over the edge.

Well I think both of you are underestimating the reader. I take credit for my idea, and I am proud of it. I believe the reader likes me, and also likes my idea. I just don't know how serious Dr. Roth is about endorsing it.

I'm still confused, and I give up in getting any answers from the reader. I also have another question. Dr. Roth keeps pestering me about being isolated. If I do take Leslie's crazy idea and start praying to my clitoris, I have a sneaking suspicion that Dr. Roth or the group is going to try to persuade me to masturbate. Now everything I hear about masturbating is that it is isolative behavior. So is this some kind of trick to keep me isolated?

Thank you for exposing this paradox. I may be reaching some humility when I appreciate that my own logical methods have failed to relieve me of my disease. I become open to suggestions that may seem absurd and contradictory to my previous beliefs. When I am prepared to put some of these suggestions into action, I try them first within the confines of therapy and recovery, and then experiment with these new methods out in the "real world."

Chapter 9

Making Amends As an Export Process

Speaking of the "real world," I think that we have been keeping the reader at a distance in another way, by talking here as if we don't have any lives outside of this book.

I find myself agreeing with you more and more, recently. I'm not entirely comfortable with that. But you're right. It seems artificial even to me to be acting as if our only purpose in life is to be engaged in witty repartee with each other.

Isn't it painful enough to have to talk about my sordid past? Why do you want me to bring up my wretched present?

Your present might not be so wretched if you were willing to take some joy in your clitoris.

Could you please get off my case with all this sex business! Dr. Roth, this is your book. Tell Bea to back off, mind her own business, and keep the focus on herself.

Actually Kelly, I suspect that recovery may be the best revenge. Perhaps you could surrender to the group's suggestion to pray to your clitoris.

And what the hell do you mean by that?

I suggest starting out simply. How long since you took a bubble bath?

Don't be ridiculous. I never took a bubble bath, even as a child.

How about starting now? It has been so helpful to me.

Didn't I tell you to butt out?

Maybe you could use some help in approaching a bubble bath.

I smell a rat.

Maybe the smelly rat needs a bath.

Look, guys. I'll do what you suggest just to get you off my back.

Maybe you're appeasing us the way you prepared to get fucked by your ex-husband.

Brace yourself, Bridget.

All right, all right. Maybe I could even imagine enjoying it.

Perhaps you are pushing yourself too hard if you expect to enjoy such a novel experience. I suggest that simply committing to having the experience would be a revolutionary change. I also want to be clear that you would be making this change on behalf of the group. If you let go of carrying the group's anhedonia, or joylessness, then the group might have to acknowledge other ways in which joy is avoided.

So what exactly are you suggesting I do?

Since you seem invested in fighting with Bea about sex and about me, I suggest you ask Bea how to proceed. Then you might call Bea before and after engaging in the dreadful experience.

You don't mind my calling you, Bea?

My pleasure.

I still think we need to let the reader in on our lives outside the group.

You are really transparent, Leslie. You just want an excuse to let the reader know that you are a psychiatrist because you think that will make you more interesting to the reader.

I'm blushing. Even though you are obviously correct, Kelly, I am somehow taking responsibility for bringing our lives outside to the reader's attention.

For you, taking responsibility is a professional hazard. But you may also be doing something more interesting here. You may be taking care of Roth's agenda, thereby relieving me of that role. My understanding is that Roth wants to explore Steps Eight and Nine in this chapter, and I cannot imagine confining the process of making amends to this group.

So that's what Dr. Roth means by an export process. That we export the work we do in group by taking the show on the road.

Which is a particularly apt metaphor in relation to your career, Warren, with your political aspirations.

What a fiasco. I came to see Dr. Roth years ago complaining about a recurrent dream that I would become a highly placed public servant. I asked him to help me get rid of this dream and he told me the only way to let go of it was to see where it took me. What kind of amends am I making by running for political office, wasting the time and money of many of my friends and family?

Sometimes you are a dumb-ass nigger. With all of your talent, IN has had to work damn hard at depreciating you to suppress your ambition and political aspirations. Running for office is an amends to yourself.

Even if you're right, Leslie, it doesn't give you the right to call me a nigger. Only I can do that to myself.

Perhaps explicitly authorizing someone else to carry the depreciating messages is another amends to yourself.

I guess you would say that is what I am doing in my work. It works in two ways. First the fact that I am working at all. My father's workaholism left me in a position to take responsibility for my alcoholic mother, so I wound up siding with her in resenting his work rather than her alcohol. So I guess you'd say that the fact that I am working at all is an amends to myself.

Even when you haven't been working, you have been an amazing husband and father. That is an amends to yourself, too.

Ouch. I'll avoid that one at the moment. Sticking with my work, I find that as a broker I am mediating between two seemingly adversarial sides all the time.

So you get to use the same skills that paralyzed you in your family of origin to be professionally successful.

I'll see your insight and raise you one. For all of your daddy's drinking and womanizing, he was one of this town's most successful black entrepreneurs. So part of what you need in order to realize your political dream is owning some of the good stuff you got from him.

This conversation about making amends seems totally foreign to me. When I hear about Steps Eight and Nine, I think about apologizing to all of those people whose lives have been ruined by my misbehavior. After all, I am the unlovable wretch that my poor ex-husband had to put up with for all those years. Don't I owe him amends for all of his suffering?

I think it's time for a joke: Clancy stops by his neighborhood pub. He goes up to the bartender and orders a pint of stout. He downs half the pint in one gulp, wipes his mouth on his sleeve, and flings the rest of the beer in the bartender's face.

"What the fuck did you do that for?" screams the astonished bartender.

Clancy shrugs, puts his mug on the bar and leaves quietly.

A few months later, Clancy returns to the pub. He approaches the bartender, who eyes him warily. Clancy orders his pint of stout, downs half the pint, wipes his mouth, and flings the rest of the beer in the bartender's face.

"You can't behave this way!" shrieks the bartender, shaking his fist at the unrepentant Clancy. "Do not set foot in this pub again until you have consulted a psychiatrist."

A few weeks later Clancy returns. As soon as he enters the pub, the bartender calls out, "So Clancy, have you seen a psychiatrist?"

"Yes sir," answers Clancy. And he orders a pint of stout, drinks half, wipes his mouth, and flings the rest in the bartender's face.

"I thought you said you saw the psychiatrist," wails the red-faced bartender.

"I did," explains Clancy. "Now I understand why I fling the beer in your face."

After all these years, you still have trouble telling a joke.

So who's flinging beer in Roth's face?

One of the major gifts of the Twelve-Step programs is the realization that recovery from addiction entails and requires broad change in the addict's behaviors and relationships with others. Insight without change does not support sobriety. The first seven steps focus mostly on the addict's relationship with self and a Higher Power that can be found within the fellowship of recovery. The Twelve-Step programs also offer a list of twelve promises, which are a concrete manifestation of the hope of recovery. These promises seem to emerge spontaneously and effortlessly as a direct consequence of working on Steps Eight and Nine.

Kelly, I need to make amends to you. Just a few paragraphs ago you were talking about your idea that making amends involves apologizing. I also had that idea when I first heard about Steps Eight and Nine at meetings. Although you may not see it in my behavior now, at one time I was highly proficient in the art of maintaining distance by apologizing for almost anything I did. I gradually realized that for me, the whole point of making a list of people I had harmed was to break my denial about what an insignificant piece of shit I am. As I made this list, I had to acknowledge that I have been important in the lives of a lot of people, including my family of origin, my wife and my children, my friends, and others. When I was more actively engaged in my addiction, I would fail to connect to people, as I failed to connect just now to you. And although you may or may not have noticed my not connecting to you, thank God I am now aware of it.

Hmm. I wonder if I have been trying to make amends to the reader during this chapter.

Well, you have certainly been clear with us how isolated you have been, both personally and professionally. I have not thought of this until now, but in some ways you are the kind of psychiatrist I imagine Bob might have become if he had ever gotten into recovery.

Thanks, Bea, I think. Though once again, I hear the group confronting me lovingly on my sabotaging the process of intimacy by being indirect in my seduction. So I hope that at least part of my wish for us to share our lives outside of the group with the reader is in the service of becoming more genuinely intimate.

What I am hearing, Leslie, is your difficulty imagining that the reader might be able to see you as a respected colleague. For me as a lawyer and aspiring politician—IN would say aspiring hypocrite and thief—I imagine that my career would be ruined if the electorate found out that I am a wacko in therapy.

I go in and out of shame about being a patient. After all, as a shrink I have the rationalization that being in therapy is a necessary part of my training. I faked my way through two analyses on that pretext. That illusion is much harder to maintain in group. And you're right, deep down I expect the reader to have contempt for me.

Do you have the same feelings about Dr. Roth? Is it hard for you to see him as a colleague, too?

Yeah, I vacillate between not believing that he can even see me or see who I am and then hearing everything he says as a criticism of me.

As the group increasingly experiences me as a colleague with whom it collaborates instead of a punitive, critical authority that it must defend itself against, the group can transfer this experience of collaboration to relationships outside of the group. The group had invested its willingness to work with me in Richard, and similarly located a part of me in the reader. The group has then assigned Leslie the task of engaging me via the reader. As the rigidity of these roles is being dismantled, the whole group is freer to work with each other and me.

Thus the process of making amends, changing one's life and relationships in recovery, brings us full circle to the experience of carrying the message of recovery as described in Chapter 2. While some people understand the process of recovery as cleaning up or restoring the addict to a previously healthy condition, I suggest that we need a different model for the process of recovery from addiction as a family disease. This different model involves understanding the making of amends as building new structure rather than wiping the tarnish off of old structure.

At this point I would like to make amends to you as the reader. I realize that in our discussion of powerlessness in Chapter 3 I failed to offer you a clear distinction between two concepts that are often confused with each other: powerlessness and helplessness. I suspect that my omission had to do with a defect of character of mine that I mentioned in Chapter 1, that is, my difficulty trusting you to perform your role as reader. Since you are still maintaining your commitment to reading, my lack of trust becomes increasingly untenable, and the distinction between powerlessness and helplessness emerges in our relationship. As I proposed in Chapter 3, I am powerless over whether you read this book. On the other hand, I am not helpless in my relationship with you as reader. I am able to ask for limitless help from amongst the social network that I am supported by. Only the illusion of my own personal power would interfere with the maintenance of the bonds that attach me to the power available outside of myself.

If you indulge me in a brief thought experiment, perhaps I can further illuminate, so to speak, this distinction between powerlessness and helplessness. Imagine that for whatever reason the sun were suddenly to be removed from existence. We are not considering an explosion or any other event that would create energy, but simply that the sun ceased to exist. Now if you are a clever physicist, you will point out that we on earth would not know of this event for about eight minutes as the last rays of this extinct sun travel the ninety-three million miles from the sun to the earth. So let us begin the thought experiment by asking the following question: What happens to us on earth eight minutes after the sun ceases to exist?

If we return to my description in Chapter 1 of the destruction of the World Trade Center, we might imagine a proportionately greater reaction from the world's population to the loss of the sun. We may picture newspaper headlines, television coverage, and international disaster planning. Or perhaps simply mass hysteria. Perhaps we wonder how long the earth would survive such a devastating loss. If we pause to consider the inevitability of our freezing to death, we might arrive at a sobering conclusion: the earth would be completely sterile almost simultaneously with the last ray of sunlight. The proponents of humanity's power may now object, protesting that we certainly have enough power to keep us warm at least for a limited period of time, even without the sun. Some simple arithmetic should loosen our grip on the illusion of self-sufficiency. The temperature in deep space is absolute zero, or zero degrees Kelvin. The earth's temperature is maintained at 400 to 500 degrees above absolute zero solely by the action of the sun. With all the fuss about global warming, scientists debate whether the sum total of all of man's activity has succeeded in raising the earth's temperature by five to ten degrees. If we were optimistically able to generate 1 percent of the energy that we get from the sun, the impact would be like trying to boil a quart of water above one lit match. Recognizing that we cannot generate the power that we depend on for our existence, we may be able to admit that we are powerless. But because we can and do depend upon the consistent and reliable availability of power from the sun we are certainly not at all helpless.

Okay, Roth, now that you have impressed the reader with your credentials as a bona fide scientist, maybe you can stop playing Feynman or Hawking and come back to your humble group.

Stop that, Richard. I was feeling some fondness again for Dr. Roth when he seemed to be waxing poetic.

You didn't hear him lecturing at you like your ex-husband?

Maybe my ex-husband's brilliant lecturing was one of the parts of him I found attractive. The lecturing only turned ugly when he started on the theme of my drinking or smoking.

I guess I also caught myself basking in the warmth of Dr. Roth's sunlight. Even if you all do tease me about adoring him.

Have you ever considered whether we are shaming you about adoring Dr. Roth or maybe you are using us to cover up your own shame about how attached you are?

I know that being needy and dependent was not something I ever was encouraged to do as a little kid.

Could it be that your willingness to be so attached to Roth is an amends you are making to yourself? Even if my flirtations with the reader are an indirect way for me to flirt with Roth, I have never been so open as I have been here about the process of being seductive. And as long as we are into making amends, Bea, I want to acknowledge your comment to me contrasting me to your previous psychiatrist, Bob. I have been hypervigilant my entire career never to be seductive to my patients. I can better appreciate now that I have appeared aloof, cold, and distant as a result. What is worse for me, though, is that I have been practicing psychiatry in a self-maintained straitjacket, probably out of fear that if I were warmer I would become intrusive and wind up with my fingers in some poor patient's ass. Since I was trained to maintain a so-called professional distance, I have been quite self-righteous about the inappropriateness of the touchy-feely types. So here is another confession. As much as I know that I needed your help, Roth, I have had contempt for your not keeping me more at a distance. I told myself that you were being seductive in sharing any of your process with me.

I would not join any club that would accept the likes of me as a member.

Yeah, yeah. But I'm not finished with the confession. So bear with me even though I'm taking up way more than my fair share of the space here.

You're the only one who is accusing you of monopolizing.

Well, what I really need to say is that I have been considering conducting a psychotherapy group myself.

Is this another attempt to seduce the reader? You think because the reader is interested in groups, you can snag the reader by doing a group.

Kelly, I will head off your next accusation at the pass. I have resisted starting a group precisely because doing so seemed like such slavish imitation of Roth. So, Bea, you are not alone in feeling shame about being attached here. And no, Kelly, at least for the moment I am not considering writing a book.

Good. I'm relieved not to have yet another party I would be obliged to show up at.

I'm sure you wouldn't want to show up in anything I wrote. We might have to get into the bubble bath together.

To follow your confessional lead, Leslie, I need to bring something to the table. IN says none of you want to hear this. I met with some key players in the

Rainbow Coalition for lunch this week. I was sure they just wanted to talk about some mundane business that I have taken a small part in. When their chief political organizer said that they have had their eye on me and they want me to consider running in the next election for a seat on the city council, I almost fell off my chair.

That's great, Warren.

But it got worse. You know my ward is hotly contested. And my opponent has been amassing a pretty sizable war chest. So I wasn't exactly looking forward to being David to this guy's Goliath.

So did the coalition commit to any financial backing for you?

That's what killed me. Turns out some of my big daddy's business friends are waiting in the wings for me to run. They have offered to contribute twenty thousand in seed money. And of course I have IN screaming at the top of his lungs that you can't trust these shiftless niggers to keep their word. Like I have lived my whole life without a sense of there being a sun to warm me, and now all of a sudden I'm blinded by the brightness, and I don't trust that it's for real. And I hear Dr. Roth's voice in my head, the prick, saying that all I need to do is show up to receive what these guys are offering. That it's not my job to determine the quality or quantity of the support.

Have you talked about this with your wife, Sheila?

Yeah, she was a little hesitant about the time commitment.

Thank God you have Sheila to introduce a little reality into this adventure.

Sheila was only a little hesitant?

Well, we talked about it some, but I still have a hard time opening up to her. I think my marriage is an area that I need to get more help with. So thanks, Leslie, for opening up the question.

Any time, Warren. That's what I meant at the beginning of the chapter when I asked what we were withholding from the reader. What we don't tell the reader we are also not working on ourselves.

One way of understanding making amends as an export process is that the goal of making amends is to establish healthy boundary regulation. If we return for a moment to our thought experiment involving the sun, we can appreciate the importance of boundary maintenance. In our dependence on the sun for energy and warmth, we clearly need to remain attached to the sun for our survival. We also have a "skin" or boundary that for the earth is the atmosphere. This atmosphere must be able to function in three ways: the energy from the sun must be allowed to pass through the atmosphere to warm the earth, the atmosphere must be able to block certain toxic radiation to protect the earth from harm, and excess energy from the earth must be exported via diffusion through the atmosphere into space. Such is the challenge for each member of our group, for the group as a whole, and for anyone in recovery. AA members may be asked by newcomers for help in utilizing the sometimes confusing, sometimes contradictory experience, strength, and hope that are available in the fellowship of recovery. Experienced AA members are likely to suggest that the newcomer "take what fits and leave the rest." This suggestion reflects an appreciation of the importance of boundary regulation in the process of recovery, and particularly the development of semi-permeable boundaries as the result of engaging in the Twelve-Step programs.

Maintaining openness to changing or amending our relationships with the world outside of us allows us to remain attached to others. Therefore making amends, like every other aspect of recovery, is a selfish process, which results in the maker of amends being changed without requiring that the object of the amends be changed at all. The only proviso offered as a guideline in the process of making amends is that no one is harmed in the process. I suggest that this guideline can be operationalized by examining whether a particular change would harm the relationship between the maker of amends and the world outside. I hope that you have seen thus far in our work together the three forms of boundary regulation described above in both the therapy group and Twelve-Step group processes we have been sharing:

1. Energy (through feelings) is received from the group by each of its members.
2. The group and each of its members are free to reject or exclude feelings or actions that might be toxic or counterproductive at that time.
3. Members of the group share feelings that are exported from the individual into the group.

You may recall a similar discussion of semipermeable boundaries in Chapter 1. I suggest that you consider how each of the members of our group, including yourself and me, engage in the exercise of boundary regulation, both individually and collectively.

By the way, reader, this suggestion of Roth is a sneaky way for him to create a segue to his next chapter on inventory and self-analysis.

Chapter 10

Continuing the Inventory
and "Self-Analysis"

Sorry about that catty remark at the end of the last chapter. I realize that I have been suppressing an issue that is painful for me.

So you were being irritable and unreasonable without knowing it.

Except that now you are able to see your own behavior and what triggers it much more quickly.

Thanks for your efforts in cheering me up, guys. I know that I have made a lot of progress here. But in a way, that is what is painful. I have a difficult piece of work to do. I think all of you, except maybe the reader, know that I have been in treatment with Roth for twenty years. I recognize that I feel some shame about being here that long, and I have achieved some acceptance of the voice in my head that tells me that it's not okay to be that needy. Roth and I have joked about growing old together, about my sending his kids to college, and my need to take care of him like I took care of my parents. I have been wondering if I have been avoiding something in not talking about leaving therapy.

I know that I have talked about wanting to leave. It seems like you all tried to push me over the edge with all that sex talk.

Kelly, your protestations are really wearing thin. Were you planning on letting the group know about your phone calls to me?

You bitch. Can't you keep anything just between the two of us?

Sorry, Kelly. Bob taught me the dangers of maintaining secrets.

You win. I have taken a bubble bath every day since Dr. Roth made the suggestion, and I have called Bea before and after the bath each time. I cannot say that I enjoy the baths, or talking to Bea for that matter. But much as I hate to admit it, and even though I get no pleasure from it, I find that I am looking forward to taking a bath. But I still don't like you, Bea.

Of course not.

Did we leave you high and dry, Richard? You were saying something about leaving that was hard for me to hear, so I could understand our rescuing you and us.

Thanks, Leslie, but I suspect that I have as much difficulty imagining leaving the bathtub as Kelly has imagining jumping into it.

You're sweet, Richard. I would miss you terribly.

Yes. That captures the conflict about termination for me. Can I plan to take an action, leaving the group, which will certainly result in my missing all of you, and Roth in particular? I have had friends drift away during the process of my treatment and recovery, but for the most part these friends needed me to stay sick. I have never had the experience of leaving an intimate relationship on good terms. A big part of me screams inside that I would have to be crazy to leave Roth. Could it really make sense to leave simply to assure myself that I am not defending myself against the feelings that come up about leaving?

Didn't you leave once before?

That was the familiar type of leaving. After graduating from business school, the consulting firm that hired me sent me on a project a few hundred miles away. I came home on weekends, but getting to appointments with Roth during the week was out of the question. So we stopped treatment, or interrupted it, depending on how clear either of us was that I would return to treatment at some point. I waited a month or two after the assignment ended before calling Roth. That was about as much ambivalence and resistance as I could muster.

It's funny, Richard, that you could see yourself as ambivalent. Your attachment to Dr. Roth seems so solid and genuine.

Thanks, Leslie. It's just that I am starting to wonder whether the security of our relationship should make it more difficult to imagine leaving.

I'm not sure how connected I am to AA, but I expect to go to meetings for the rest of my life.

Good analogy, Kelly. For myself I have noticed that while I continue to go to meetings, I am much less compulsive about it than I used to be.

Same for me. I was so hungry for support when I hit bottom that I would go to two meetings every day. I had a list of a hundred people to call. Dr. Roth confronted me on using meetings and people in the fellowship like drugs of abuse. I was doing a heroic amount of work and not succeeding in taking in much of the benefit. I should also acknowledge that even more recently, I decided to go to AA meetings even though I do not consider myself an alcoholic. I rationalized this action based on there being "better recovery" in AA. Dr. Roth confronted me again on going to AA meetings while I continued to drink.

Dr. Roth tried to control your drinking?

Doesn't sound like the Roth I know.

He didn't really take a position on my drinking. He just pointed out that since the criterion for group membership in AA is a desire to stop drinking, and I wasn't even letting the group know that I was drinking, I was setting myself up not to experience belonging to the group.

Thanks again, Leslie. You capture the message with my anxiety. That accusing voice in my head tells me that there remains at least one more piece of work that I would need to do here for me to be able to leave treatment honestly.

Like an honorable discharge?

As opposed to a foul discharge?

As I described in Chapter 9, we realize the promises of recovery in a changed, or amended, relationship with the world outside of ourselves. The last three steps are called maintenance steps in that they support us in maintaining our lives in the attached mode that was impossible while we were invested in controlling our lives with addiction. The form of attachment is now functional, adaptive, and mutual rather than toxic and parasitic. AA members, joking about themselves, may declare, "Alcoholics don't have relationships; they take hostages." Likewise, Al-Anon members may describe themselves as not having relationships, but maintaining caseloads.

I suggest that good-enough therapy or good-enough work on Steps One through Nine enables us to partake of a social system that we neither have to hold hostage nor turn into a burdensome caseload. Such an environment offers abundant opportunities to continue our self-examination by providing loving intimate feedback accompanied by feelings expressed directly and without shaming.

Were you making fun of me with that remark about a foul discharge?

Hunh?

Well, you know how much shame I feel about anything to do with sex. And how humiliated I felt admitting here that I would sometimes get wet down there when I saw Dr. Roth individually. So I feel hurt and angry that you would accuse me of having foul discharges.

Sometimes the voice in your head makes IN look like a pussycat. Oops. Did I just set myself up to be accused of making fun of you again, Kelly?

Maybe we are poking fun at Kelly. I wouldn't be surprised if we were all just a little anxious about her threat of enjoying a bubble bath.

You're probably correct, Leslie. I am still struggling with the idea of Richard leaving. One question I have is, why now?

You know, I hadn't thought of that. And I know Roth is smiling inside, saying to himself, "Good work, Richard. You don't have to be vigilant in searching out all of your motives before you talk about your feelings and impulses." Anyway, your question, Bea, leads me to wonder whether my umbilical connection to Roth has me identifying with some feelings he has about this being Chapter 10, and this book coming to an end soon.

Good work, Richard. I do feel sad when I consider that I am in the process of completing this book. I acknowledge the important role you play in this book, and at the same time I support you in examining what you need right now. That examination of your needs in the present is the foundation for your continuing to do your own inventory work or "self-analysis."

So if I make my staying or leaving contingent on the timing of your finishing this book, I have repeated my childhood experience of my needs being subordinated to taking care of my parent's unstated needs.

Exactly. And then this book, as an extension of me, would be holding you hostage.

So I need to decide when I leave based on my own needs.

Yes.

I'd like to change the subject.

Come on, Warren. You know as well as we do that there is no such thing as changing the subject because we are always on the same subject, which is all of us.

Yes, Bea. I think I threw in that comment to distract me from my own anxiety about Richard leaving. You have been an incredible gift in my life, buddy.

Now I am feeling anxious receiving all this love. Maybe that is part of what scares me about leaving. I can see myself taking responsibility for you missing me and telling myself I am being bad.

Deal with it.

I love you too, Leslie. So what's on your mind, Warren?

I'll trust that I am not colluding in creating a distraction for you and the group. I wanted to revisit my relationship with Sheila. I talked with her further about the potential for me to run for political office. It looks like the real problem is not politics. Sheila said I have been more distant from her over the past few years. Personally, I think we have been distant for longer than that, but my standards for what constitutes intimacy have changed during the time I have been going to meetings and being in this group.

It sounds like Sheila feels that you're holding back in relationship to her.

Maybe. But why would you say that?

What is my motive, or based on what information?

Both.

My motive, because I care about you. And the information is in the group, as Dr. Roth has told us so often. I see you as having withheld from the group that your marriage lacks intimacy, and your withholding such an important dynamic from the group suggests to me that you have not been intimate with us.

Kind of like not talking about drinking at an AA meeting?

Look who's decided to join the group. And as long as Kelly is jumping to your defense, Warren, I smell another form of withholding. How long since you and Sheila made love?

You don't have to answer that question, Warren.

Thanks for your support, Kelly, but I don't think I want you as my attorney here. It's been a while.

You may not want my counsel, counselor, but methinks you are tightening the noose around your neck with every answer. I think Leslie is onto something here, and the vagueness of "It's been a while" is another indication of holding out on us.

Leslie and Richard are right. And I was wrong to reject your help, Kelly. I can see that I am really not ready to be clearer with you and therefore be more intimate with you, or more intimate with Sheila, for that matter.

Too late, my friend. In making this admission honestly, you just became more intimate with us.

The group is demonstrating two ways in which we can continue the process of taking our inventory. One way is to use the people with whom we share the most intimacy, and either solicit their feedback or more often simply welcome what they share with us as a way to maintain a loving mirror of who we are and how we are functioning on a day-to-day basis. We also need to be gentle with our inventory work, and practice this gentleness by not doing this "self-analysis" under pressure.

I don't know how this is connected, Warren, but your talking about how your relationship with Sheila helps you look at your difficulty with work and intimacy reminds me of how my relationship with Russ has transformed my vision not only of sex but food and money as well. You all know that I lost about one hundred pounds over the first few years that I was in Overeaters Anonymous. Wait a second. I'm having a senior moment. I don't think I have shared that with our reader. Sorry. I wonder if my relationship with Russ, and Dr. Roth, has also helped me to see how I unwittingly exclude people. Maybe there is more anxiety and shame about my transformation than I have appreciated. Anyway, for the next ten years it seemed like nothing I did or didn't do in OA would make a dent in the last forty pounds that separated me from the goal weight that had been set by my nutritionist. I prayed about it, wrote out several inventories, even talked with Dr. Roth about the possibility that I chose an anorexic nutritionist. The only thing I didn't do was admit that I was lonely. Living with and then getting married to Russ gave me an opportunity to share the intimacy of eating together. I was amazed to find that he cooks at least as well as I do, and I have been willing to let go of controlling when I eat and how I eat as well as letting go of how much I eat, which was really all that my abstinence from overeating had involved up until that point. So I found myself losing weight again.

I must say that I noticed you were getting thinner. I felt afraid that you might be sick or something.

I wondered about you as well. I remembered that you have had a couple of cancer scares and I thought how tragic it would be to get sick when you are happily married for the first time after so many years.

I'm all choked up. I get it that you really love me and care about me. I haven't been preoccupied with medical illness in a while. And you have been holding that for me.

I hate to be a party pooper, Bea, but I don't think you have let go of all of your anxiety about physical illness.

Thanks for reminding me, Warren. I must confess that I have been worrying about Russ's health. He has taken a couple of nasty spills recently.

So maybe you are planning to lose Russ the way I am planning to lose Roth.

I expressed some sadness a few pages back about my anticipating the end of this book. I was brief in my comment and I realize at the moment that the loss that connects most directly to my sadness is the loss of contact with you, the reader. So out of respect for Richard, and perhaps to give him the space not to have to be responsible for monitoring my defenses, I acknowledge that the following examination of losses may relate to the impending loss of our relationship of author to reader.

Thanks, Roth.

You're welcome, Richard.

The inventory work that takes place as part of Step Four described in Chapter 7 is simply a cataloging of all of the aspects of ourselves, including parts that are adaptive and functional and parts that are destructive and dysfunctional. Although I condensed the examination of Step Five into that discussion of inventory work, I suggest that the processes of examining oneself compassionately and sharing the inventory with another human being, a Higher Power and oneself are two separable events. The separate nature of creating an inventory and sharing it is analogous to the distinction between having a dream and sharing the dream in treatment with all of its associations. But even when the dream is analyzed with all of its associations, change is not automatic. Even if we believe that our friend Clancy in Chapter 9 understands why he flings beer in the bartender's face, his understanding alone does not stop the behavior.

Step Six involves becoming entirely ready to have a Power greater than ourselves remove our defects of character. When we look from the outside at another person's addiction and witness the destruction and havoc wrought by the disease, we might naively assume that the removal of the addiction with all of its roots would be a procedure to be welcomed by the addict. If we identify more closely, however, we might recognize that if addiction is a family disease, then removing the addiction is likely to be experienced as being robbed of a family heirloom.

Therefore, in addition to humility and working through, the process of letting go of addiction entails the willingness to embrace ongoing losses. Arguably, the most difficult loss for the addict in recovery is the loss of self-sufficiency. Whatever the content of the amends undertaken in Steps Eight and Nine, the process of making amends is a concrete indication that the addict acknowledges needing to be attached and connected to other human beings in order to recover. The process of continuing to work on a personal inventory on a daily basis accomplishes the task of identifying the parts of ourselves that might usefully be surrendered in the service of becoming more intimately attached to others. Because the making of amends enriches the social system that is available to support this inventory work, the "self-analysis" that occurs is really a group analysis of the self and not an analysis by oneself.

So to return for a moment to our relationship, I prepare to let go of our relationship at the end of this book. I can appreciate the loss, trusting that if we have established a good enough connection, that when we need each other sometime in the future, we will be available to each other. Our subsequent contact might entail my writing another book, or I might become the reader of a book you have written. In this way our relationship stands in contrast with my relationship with the other members of our group who have authorized me to be their therapist in addition to being the writer of this book.

I guess that means I could leave treatment and trust myself that I would return when I needed to.

And I can stay in treatment and let go of needing to be the psychiatrist for Dr. Roth or the reader.

I would like to conclude this chapter with a meditation on optimal distance. Again, out of respect for Richard, I acknowledge up front that this meditation prepares us for Chapter 11 titled "Prayer and Meditation As Group Analytic Functions."

Thanks again, Dr. Roth.

You're welcome again, Richard.

Optimal distance is a concept that describes the manner in which a system of two or more people regulates the intensity of their interactions and relationships. In theory, when the distance in a relationship becomes too small, the boundary regulation of the people involved suffers from attempts to control what would otherwise be autonomous actions. The member of the dyad or group who assumes the role of needing the most distance may experience being engulfed, overtaken, and suffocated. Likewise when the distance in a relationship increases, the members of the dyad or group may suffer from the loss of nourishment and support that had been obtained from the relationship up until the point that the distance had increased. Then the person who is elected to take on the role of being needy may make attempts to reduce the distance by clinging in response to the experience of being rejected or abandoned.

If we return to the metaphor in Chapter 9 of our relationship with the sun, and we imagine that instead of a catastrophic loss of the sun that the sun moves toward or away from us, then we may develop a useful physical image of optimal distance. We generally take for granted that our distance from the sun guarantees a range of temperature on earth that supports life. We understand that if the earth's orbit were reduced to that of Venus, the intrusion of increased energy from the sun would probably destroy all but the most heat-tolerant life on Earth. Likewise if we became as distant from the sun as Mars, the reduced availability of solar energy would result in most if not all of life on earth freezing to death. So not only do we depend on the existence of the sun, but we are also critically dependent on the maintenance of optimal distance from the sun.

A group that is carrying the message of recovery as defined in Chapter 2, whether that group is a Twelve-Step group, psychotherapy group, or a healthy family, has the capacity to effortlessly and automatically maintain optimal distance among its members. This capacity arises as a direct consequence of the group's awareness of and attention to its own process as described in that chapter. To anticipate Chapter 11, the means whereby the group achieves this awareness and attention to its own process is through prayer and meditation.

What I would like to draw your attention to now, though, is the exquisite role that Step Ten, continuing the personal inventory, has in the maintenance of optimal distance. One way of understanding how to use other people in the elaboration of this continuing inventory is to focus on two questions in connection to each significant relationship in our lives:

1. Have I intruded nonconsensually into this person's life in order to control the relationship?
2. Have I run away from or set up barriers against this person in order to isolate myself from the relationship?

You may recognize that these general questions describe the two polar opposite roles of addiction as a family disease. The codependent role invariably entails some kind of physical or emotional intrusion into the life of the addict. The addict role conversely creates distance and isolation. I hope that our work thus far demonstrates the futility of attempting to answer the above questions all by ourselves. Left to my own devices, I am unlikely to know whether I have intruded nonconsensually into your life or created distance between us. Only through sharing our experience with each other can I hope to gain an accurate perspective concerning the impact of my behavior on our relationship.

Chapter 11

The Development of Prayer
and Meditation
As Group Analytic Functions

I felt hurt, Richard, when you and Dr. Roth were flirting with each other at the end of the last chapter.

Maybe your own difficulty flirting keeps you at that optimal distance Dr. Roth was describing. That probably applies to me, too.

My flirting has always been mixed with so much shame it's been hard for me to use it to get closer.

I remember how shocked I was when Dr. Roth asked me if I ever flirted with the people that I met at Twelve-Step meetings. With all the talk about God, I associated meetings with going to church as a kid. That meant being serious and solemn and being punished if I was bad.

I grew up without any religion and I have just as much difficulty imagining flirting at an AA meeting. Besides, wouldn't that be thirteenth stepping?

In case you don't already know, reader, thirteenth stepping is two members of a Twelve-Step meeting getting together for a romantic or sexual relationship, usually when one or both of them has very little experience in recovery.

Sort of like you seducing the reader?

I could get defensive about that comment, Kelly, but not in this chapter.

So I assumed that there were rules of conduct in meetings, that I was responsible for maintaining a dignified decorum. Partly I got that idea from the suggestion at meetings that we not engage in cross-talk.

The spookiest part of my first meeting was the way people talked. Of course I was silent in meetings for most of my first year in recovery. In my head I was still at the dinner table as a little kid. With all of the fussing from my brothers and sisters when Daddy wasn't around, and with Daddy holding forth when he managed to show up for dinner, I never got a word in edgewise. I couldn't imagine how a group of people could all talk without interrupting each other and competing for limited airtime.

Are you okay, Richard? You seem kind of quiet.

Yeah. I'm fine. Not ready to leave the group yet, if that's what you were wondering. I suspect that in Roth's lingo I was meditating.

That's another thing about Twelve-Step meetings. People talking about doing stuff that's either weird like meditating, or like the Holy Rollers I grew up with praying all the time. When I did some Transcendental Meditation after college my family thought I had gone off the deep end. They accused me of selling out to some Indian cult, but they couldn't figure out whether that was better or worse than my taking up with a white girlfriend for a while.

You never mentioned a white girlfriend.

Does Sheila know about that?

You've got to stop painting yourself into corners, Warren. I can't be saving your ass all the time.

It's your fault, Richard. You had to bring up that meditation shit.

The group appreciates the risk of engaging in prayer and meditation. If we understand prayer as speaking to the group conscience, or Higher Power of the group, and meditation as listening to the group conscience, then prayer and meditation inexorably bring us into closer conscious contact with that Higher Power.

Roth, you are a shameless pimp for Twelve-Step tripe.

Perhaps you learned more in your meditation than you are comfortable sharing.

Okay, you got me. I was thinking about my role in the group, and particularly about my relationship to you. How the group, largely through Kelly, but also by consensus, designates me as your favorite. I realize that I have occupied a similar role in my family, where I experience myself as a usurper. I get all these good things in my life: money, a wife and family, a developing career. So why am I in therapy? Why am I not just satisfied and happy with what I have? I hear the group questioning whether I deserve to take up space here, as if I have to kill someone else here to have a chair to sit in. And then I realize that I grew up in the shadow of my dead older sister. Even to describe her that way seems strange. Edie died when she was a year old of SIDS, crib death. Before I was born. But somehow I have held myself responsible for her death. Mother made it clear that if Edie had lived that Emily and I would never have been conceived, because she really wanted to stop after having a girl.

You have done well in creating a balance between speaking and listening as a way to find space for yourself in this group.

Don't think you can appease me with your cheesy affirmations.

Well, I'll take Dr. Roth's affirmation for myself even if he meant it for you.

How interesting that the group would assume that my prayers were intended for the ears of one member only.

Even if you are speaking to all of us, Dr. Roth, I don't see how you and the reader can be included in creating the balance between speaking and listening. After all, in writing this book you are ultimately responsible for all of the speaking or praying, and the reader is limited to the role of listening or meditating.

Excellent point, Leslie.

Uh-oh, Leslie. Can't you see this one coming? You just gave Roth the ammunition to confront you on your flirtation with the reader as a displacement from flirting with him.

Do I need to take that seriously?

Up to you, Leslie. I am aware that you, as members of the group who both speak and listen, have the opportunity to function more fully in creating a group conscience. The authority and responsibility that you and the reader give me to write this book is a mirror image of the freedom that the reader has to observe and listen without constraints.

All of this chatter about talking and listening is making my head spin.

Are you sure it's the chatter and not other recent developments?

God, Bea, what now?

Just seems like your phone call last night might be significant.

Do you really want me to regret calling you? I give up. I was taking a bubble bath last night, minding my own business, Bea, and out of nowhere I started talking to my clitoris.

And I was counting on you to help me stay sane in this loony bin!

Sorry, Warren. It just came over me. I was thinking "what is it that I would like to hear from Dr. Roth?" And I realized I wanted him to say, "Kelly, I'm sorry I have been ignoring you." And I realized that all my life I have pretended my clitoris wasn't there. So, thinking to myself that I am going stark raving, I am sitting in the bathtub and I say "Clitoris, I'm sorry I have been ignoring you." And then I was stupid enough to share the insanity with the bitch.

You're leaving out the best part.

I promise I am going to kill you.

Careful what you pray for.

Yeah, Kelly. You wouldn't want us to really understand how intense the love between you and Bea is.

Backstabbers! You win. I am completely humiliated. I had the fantasy that my clitoris was listening to me.

Well, now I've heard everything. A meditating pussy.

Have you all ever given any thought to how we work together here in group?

What do you mean, Bea?

Two pieces. First I was reflecting on how we manage to do the work we need to accomplish together. Like the comment you made at the beginning of this chapter. When I first went to OA, everyone mentioned food but everyone seemed to have different issues with food and different ways in which our relationships with food made our lives unmanageable. There were overeaters like me, but also anorexics and bulimics. Some people's comments would focus on the impact of the disease on a relationship, sometimes marriage, sometimes parents, sometimes children. Only after a few years was I able to see that what we were sharing at meetings was all connected, that basic themes were being expressed and carried by each of us working together. And even though our conversations here seem equally, if not more, disjointed, sometimes I realize that Warren's distance from Sheila is my distance from Russ; Kelly's contempt for her sexuality is what I tried to do to myself by eating compulsively; Richard's ambivalence about being Dr. Roth's favorite is an expression of my ambivalence; Leslie's attempts to fix, manage, and control have been a favorite way for me to avoid being vulnerable.

Good aim, Bea. You shot all of us with a precision that should leave Roth envious. What's the second piece?

That has to do with your comment about taking up space in group. I have noticed at meetings and in this group that sometimes a person will go into a long-winded harangue while others are doing their best to blend into the woodwork. What amazes me is that gradually, without any effort, monopolizers can learn how to listen and wallflowers develop the capacity to speak.

I know what you mean. I have gone to meetings where the chairperson used a kitchen timer to regulate the length of people's comments. At first it annoyed the shit out of me. I thought if someone needed to share something, who gave the chairperson the right to set arbitrary time limits? So I found myself alternately timing my own comments precisely to the second to comply with the timer, and then spitefully and resentfully going over time to test how long it took for the chairperson to interrupt me.

Have you done the same thing with Roth's authority?

Thank you and fuck you, Richard. I guess that means yes to both Dr. Roth's authority and your authority.

I'm touched.

See, I can flirt with you as well as Dr. Roth and the reader.

Have you ever wondered why people bother to get together to pray? I used to wonder that when Momma took us to church as kids. After all, if we were supposed to be praying to God, why couldn't we do that at home without having to get all dressed up in our Sunday finest? And then maybe Daddy could have prayed with us, because he didn't come to church all that often.

That's what I meant about our working together in group. Something happens here when we share our experiences.

And need each other.

Are you speaking just for us, Dr. Roth? Because frankly, I don't see much indication that you need us.

Kelly, sometimes you can be so dense. And how do you imagine that Roth could be writing this book if it weren't for us?

But the reader doesn't know that. For all the reader knows, we could be figments of Dr. Roth's imagination.

And isn't that what you have done to yourself, Kelly, like you used to do with your clitoris, obliterate yourself by telling yourself that you or your clitoris exists only in someone else's mind?

Sometimes you guys get way too complex for me. All I need to know that I exist is one good look at my own black butt.

I wonder if Kelly is speaking on behalf of some doubts that the group has about the existence of the reader.

Pretty good, Roth. You're right. We have as much evidence of the reader's existence as the reader has of ours.

I guess it would not be surprising if we invested the reader with God-like powers to determine the integrity and authenticity of our identities.

Cut the intellectual shit, Leslie, and go back to your blatant seduction.

I won't let you pin all of this on me. You brought up the reader this time.

Whether or not the reader exists, I would like for all of us, including the reader, to go back to another meeting.

Always pushing people to go to meetings.

Don't blame Bea for this one. Roth has planned a meeting for Chapter Twelve for us to talk about the traditions.

Dr. Roth didn't come to the Twelve-Step meeting. Is he coming to the meeting in Chapter Twelve?

Don't ask me; ask Roth.

Well, Dr. Roth, are you coming to the meeting? Because if you aren't, then this chapter is the last time in this book we get to have your help.

Any thoughts or feelings about me attending the meeting?

I don't care.

You're welcome to be there if you want. After all, it's your book.

My first response was that I would feel hurt if you weren't there. Then I realized that with you at the meeting, my relationship with you would be even more complicated than it already is. I am already your patient, we are colleagues in several professional organizations, we both are conducting therapy groups, and we both are committed to recovery using the Twelve Steps. All of these connections are challenging enough for me to face without adding one more complexity of being at the same Twelve-Step meeting.

Thank you, Leslie. As Richard indicated, I was hoping that the group would hold another meeting in Chapter Twelve to talk about your experience of how the Twelve Traditions have affected your recovery in Twelve-Step programs. By the way, I acknowledge Richard's letting go of speaking on my behalf in regard to whether I would attend this meeting. I had not, in fact, intended to be present. I therefore would also like to acknowledge your progress, Leslie, in recognizing that increasing the complexity of our relationship may interfere with genuine intimacy. We might see the foreshadowing of this recognition in Chapter Seven when you shared your experience of the dual relationship with your uncle the chiropractor. You made this revelation right after attending the Twelve-Step meeting with the group in Chapter Six. I also wonder whether my abstaining from attending the meetings in Chapters Six and Twelve is an amends to Kelly.

There you go again, justifying your neglect and avoidance of me with Twelve-Step rationalizations.

I guess this means I don't get to leave the group before the end of the book.

Thanks for the reminder, Richard. I also wondered whether I was planning to absent myself from Chapter Twelve to avoid participating in my own termination work with the book and with the reader, so I'm grateful that the group is alert to engaging in the work of termination now.

I am touched by another aspect of your not joining us for Chapter Twelve. You are supporting us in having a relationship with the reader that is independent of you. You trust us enough to not have to play the role of chaperone.

That trust can be a double-edged sword, Leslie. Sometimes when my parents claimed to be trusting me they really didn't give a damn or were too preoccupied with their own shit to take a more active interest in what I was doing.

Like they trusted you when you were doing Transcendental Meditation or going out with the white girl?

Yeah. I guess that apathetic form of trust was also laced with a healthy dose of resentment.

When I was thirteen, my parents sent me halfway across the country by myself on a train to visit my older brother who was at a boarding school for disturbed adolescents. Before I arrived he had run away from school for the umpteenth time. I called my parents asking what I should do. They said to hang out at the school for a week and return home as planned. So I wound up staying in the dorm that week and had a fling with one of the kids at the school.

Are you sure that you aren't experiencing just a little neglect and abandonment by Roth?

I suppose I might feel it stronger if I weren't sure that I would have you around to remind me of him.

Leslie, you are helping me understand more about the craziness between me and my ex-psychiatrist, Bob. As if it weren't enough to be sexually abused, I also became attached to him, but like I was attached to food rather than to a person. One bite of Bob was too much, and no amount of him was ever really enough. I will miss you, Dr. Roth, when we stop seeing you in this book.

I would also like to add to what you were saying, Leslie, about our relationships to one another. When I was a kid, I can now see that I had very little relationship with my siblings. Even now, maybe especially now, it's hard for me to see past their envy of the good things in my life. A large part of what made my attaching to my siblings difficult was how much space in our family was occupied by mom's drinking. I remember reading Prince of Tides and seeing in my mind as clear as the movie, the mother telling each of her kids that they were her favorite, but telling each of them they had to keep their special status a secret from their siblings. Thank God our competition for Roth's attention is out in the open. I hope I can be as honest and intimate with my siblings someday as I am with this motley bunch.

Hey, bro, have you noticed that when you get close to being sentimental you always retreat with just a bit of irony?

You weren't supposed to notice, and if you noticed, you weren't supposed to say anything.

Just like our old family rules, huh?

Except the fucked-up part is that the old rules don't work anymore.

Like the rule that micks and niggers can't get along with each other in this town, much less be openly affectionate with each other.

Two men, no less.

Sorry to interrupt your love affair, guys, but I didn't finish my story. I left out the worst part.

And you think we want to hear it?

Exactly my point. When I realized that I could imagine that my clitoris was listening to me, I also knew that all of you would listen to me. That you have in fact been listening to me, in spite of all my ranting and raving.

Would you be disappointed to learn that you haven't been all that successful in driving us away with your so-called ranting and raving?

I guess so. Like Warren was confronting Richard on maintaining just enough distance to avoid sentimentality. And in my heart I know that your edge, Richard, is one of the parts of you I love the most. I think you're cute and funny.

In letting go of using me to maintain distance, the group increases its capacity to love and support each of its members. I am not seen as a savior or ogre, but as a valuable resource, which is the way that you become freer to experience each other.

As trusted servants.

To anticipate our discussion of the Traditions.

Bea, when you spoke earlier about missing Dr. Roth in Chapter Twelve, I wasn't in touch with feeling sad. Having been through two lengthy psychoanalyses, I thought I understood something about termination. But each of those analyses I left because we were clearly at an impasse. So when I left each time my major feeling was relief that I could stop banging my head against a wall. I get it, Richard, that you are considering leaving treatment. You have been the most challenging member of the group for me to learn from, probably because you see through my shit and have the audacity to call me on it. I know that I am not ready to leave, and yet I see that I have made some progress because in addition to the relief I imagine in not being confronted by you, I feel sad about the prospect of not seeing you in this intimate setting.

There you go again; now you are making a play for Richard. I just declared my love for him, and now you have to take him for yourself, just like my mother. She had to be the center of the universe, never leaving me any room to have any friends. Whenever I brought a friend home, she would capture them with witty conversation. My friends all thought I had a great mother because their mothers never talked to them, but they never understood that she was stealing them from me.

Speaking of feeling relieved at not banging our heads against the wall! Kelly, I am so happy that you let us in on how you get triggered by our interactions, and that your jealousy does not come from nowhere. It sounds like your mother was as lonely as you are.

What a choice for you, Kelly. To become your suicidally depressed father or your needy parasitic mother. Kind of like my Hobson's choice of distant workaholic father or pathetic alcoholic mother.

I guess the disease in my family made it difficult for me to see Daddy or Momma as a valued resource, like Dr. Roth was saying.

Maybe I could also add that I have tried hard to be in the savior role to make up for the lack of protection I experienced from my parents.

Maybe it's been hard for us to let Roth protect us and trust that he will provide a safe place here in this book.

I am feeling afraid of not having him with us in Chapter Twelve.

On the other hand, he is not clinging to us the way Kelly's mother snagged her friends.

I feel angry and hurt that you are abandoning us, Dr. Roth. You have been at meetings with me before. Why can't you come again?

I hear the group saying good-bye for now, and that the group will miss me. I acknowledge my own sadness in saying good-bye to you, the reader. I am grateful for your commitment to your role in observing our work. I hope that you will find the group helpful and enlightening in understanding how the Twelve Traditions guide our work here, in group psychotherapy, and in recovery.

At the risk of relapsing into my role of enabling my absent parents by taking care of everyone, I volunteer to chair the meeting in Chapter Twelve.

Chapter 12

The Twelve Traditions:
Boundaries and Containment

Hi. My name is Bea and I am a grateful member and the chairperson for this meeting of Al-Anon.

Hi, Bea!

Hi, everyone. Let's start with a moment of silence followed by the Serenity Prayer.

God, grant me the serenity to accept the things I cannot change, courage to change the things I can, and wisdom to know the difference.

We welcome you to the Carrying the Message Al-Anon Family Group and hope you will find in this fellowship the help and friendship we have been privileged to enjoy.

We who live, or have lived, with the problem of alcoholism understand as perhaps few others can. We, too, were lonely and frustrated, but in Al-Anon we discover that no situation is really hopeless and that it is possible for us to find contentment, and even happiness, whether the alcoholic is still drinking or not.

We urge you to try our program. It has helped many of us find solutions that lead to serenity. So much depends on our own attitudes, and *as we learn to place our problem in its true perspective, we find it loses its power to dominate our thoughts and our lives.*

The family situation is bound to improve as we apply the Al-Anon ideas. Without such spiritual help, living with an alcoholic is too much for most of us. Our thinking becomes distorted by trying to force solutions, and we become irritable and unreasonable without knowing it.

The Al-Anon program is based on the Twelve Steps (adapted from Alcoholics Anonymous), which we try, little by little, one day at a time, to apply to our lives, along with our slogans and the Serenity Prayer. The loving interchange of help among members and daily reading of Al-Anon literature thus make us ready to receive the priceless gift of serenity.

Al-Anon is an anonymous fellowship. Everything that is said here, in the group meeting and member-to-member, must be held in confidence. Only in this way can we feel free to say what is in our minds and hearts, for this is how we help one another in Al-Anon.[*]

Would someone like to read the Al-Anon Preamble to the Twelve Steps?

Hi. I'm Leslie, recovering Al-Anon.

Hi, Leslie!

The Al-Anon Family Groups are a fellowship of relatives and friends of alcoholics who share their experience, strength, and hope in order to solve their common problems. We believe alcoholism is a family illness and that changed attitudes can aid recovery.

Al-Anon is not allied with any sect, denomination, political entity, organization, or institution; does not engage in any controversy; neither endorses nor opposes any cause. There are no dues for membership. Al-Anon is self-supporting through its own voluntary contributions.

---

[*]From Al-Anon/Alateen Service Manual, 2002. Reprinted by permission of Al-Anon Family Group Headquarters, Inc.

Al-Anon has but one purpose: to help families of alcoholics. We do this by practicing the Twelve Steps, by welcoming and giving comfort to families of alcoholics, and by giving understanding and encouragement to the alcoholic.*

Thanks, Leslie. Today we are having a topic meeting and we are going to focus on the Twelve Traditions. I will give a lead on the First Tradition and then open the meeting for sharing. Before we begin let me remind us that this meeting lasts for 21 pages, so that we be mindful of the space we take in sharing. Also that we do not engage in cross-talk, give advice or make comments about one another's sharing. So, I am still Bea.

Hi, Bea!

I want to talk about the First Tradition from three perspectives. First, I'll read the Tradition. Tradition One: "Our common welfare should come first; personal progress for the greatest number depends upon unity."

One way for me to practice unity at the moment is to give this lead in the traditional manner: to tell you how I got here, what I found here, and what I am doing now in my recovery. So I'll tell you about the meaning of the First Tradition in my disease, how I have seen this Tradition at work in Al-Anon, and how I am applying this Tradition in my program today.

I didn't experience any unity in my family when I was a kid. My dad traveled on business all the time, and we didn't find out until I grew up that he had kept a mistress for years in another city. My grandmother and great-grandmother lived with us, and I didn't see any unity among them either. Each of them would fill me up with resentments they had about the other two, and the constant flow of alcohol

---

*From Suggested Preamble to the Twelve Steps, 1984. Reprinted by permission of Al-Anon Family Group Headquarters, Inc.

did not help matters either. All I ever wanted was some peace in the family, and I thought I could create that peace by myself.

When I married my first husband I was no better equipped to be in an intimate committed relationship than my parents were. This time I was the one to be unfaithful, with my psychiatrist no less, who had also seen us together as a couple. So much for unity in that therapy.

So the idea of strangers coming together with singleness of purpose yet retaining separate identities was a total mystery to me. I spent several years in Twelve-Step meetings figuring out ways to improve their effectiveness and efficiency. It took a while to sink in that the unity of the program freed me from the responsibility of fixing anyone else. I understand now that the common welfare includes my own welfare, and I am not a well person when I am fixing everyone else. I have also learned that when I allow other people to help me, together we can arrive at solutions to common problems that I would never have imagined by myself.

I'll tell you about a conflict that came up for me at an Al-Anon meeting recently. This meeting takes place in the rectory of a local church. A blind woman came to the meeting for the first time accompanied by her Seeing Eye dog. Now, I am deathly allergic to dogs. I went into a tailspin. If I protested about allowing the dog into the meeting I was a horribly insensitive bitch who would be responsible for alienating this poor blind woman from Al-Anon meetings for the rest of her life. Yet if I ignored my own needs, wasn't I spiraling into a codependent relapse by endangering my own health? By the way, did I mention that when I was a kid I had severe eczema, and my pediatrician told my parents that they had to get rid of the dog? After leaving the doctor, my parents announced that they would rather get rid of me, and proceeded to find a doctor who would cover me from head to toe with coal tar rather than have our family let go of the dog. So maybe I'm still a little angry about that.

Anyway, back to the Al-Anon meeting. I timidly raised my hand at the beginning of the meeting to share my concern for my health with the person chairing the meeting. The chairperson thought a moment and reminded the group about the first tradition. Another member who knew the layout of the church asked whether the blind woman would be comfortable with her dog staying in an adjacent room. She responded that she was actually relieved and grateful for the group providing space for her dog in such a way that the dog would not distract her during the meeting. So together we arrived at a solution that no single one of us could have achieved alone. With that I pass.

Thanks, Bea!

Thanks, everyone. The floor is now open for sharing.

Hi. My name is Warren, and I am a recovering Al-Anon.

Hi, Warren!

Thanks for your lead, Bea. I would like to talk about the Second Tradition, and I like your idea of sharing how the Tradition was missing in my past, how I found it working in recovery, and what role it plays in my life today. So Tradition Two: "For our group purpose there is but one authority—a loving God as He may express Himself in our group conscience. Our leaders are but trusted servants; they do not govern."

I'll start by saying that I did grow up in a religious family where we were taught about God in the usual Christian sense. What I can see now is that the white fellow with the beard was not really the Higher Power that we worshipped as a family. We had two gods to pay homage to, Daddy's business and Momma's pills. Any decisions that we made ultimately reflected on the needs of Daddy's demanding schedule or Momma's need to medicate her resentment about being left alone to take care of us. And then if Momma dared to let out any feelings, we could count on another god to appear in the form of Daddy's drinking.

Momma's anger often came out sideways. Once when Daddy was out of town on business, Momma decided that us kids needed a dog. We were ecstatic at the time, even though now it seems weird that we all knew and we all ignored that Daddy was always real skittish around dogs, like he was terrified of being bitten but too ashamed to let his fear show. So when Daddy came home to find a puppy with us, he got rip-roaring drunk, raging out of control, kicking the dog and threatening to give Momma a beating she wouldn't forget.

I got a clear message that night that you never wanted to cross Daddy. The fight between them escalated to the point where Daddy had taken his old service revolver out, waving it around and pointing it at the dog and then at Momma. I was listening to their screaming and finally got out of bed, ran to Daddy, and begged him not to hurt anyone. Momma grabbed me as she crumpled on the floor, sobbing and wailing as she held me in front of her. I felt so sorry for her that I didn't understand until getting into recovery that she was using me as a human shield.

When I got into recovery and came to Al-Anon meetings, every once in a while the group would need to make a decision about something. The chairperson would announce during the meeting that the group would be taking a "group conscience" about whatever needed deciding. Whether it was who was going to be the next chairperson or treasurer, whether we should give some of our Seventh Tradition money to the district office or the World Services office, or any other issue, we would always hold a group conscience. The procedure seemed ludicrous. Didn't we all have bigger problems that we needed to talk about than where to send a few lousy bucks? I complained to my sponsor about all this time wasted in meetings determining the group conscience to make trivial decisions. My sponsor gingerly asked me about how decisions were made in my family. Then I remembered about the dog, and I began to appreciate that the process of negotiating decisions together might be a lot more important than the actual content of the decision.

All of this is becoming much more relevant recently. I am considering a position in public service. I am realizing that I need to have a lot of help making the decision whether to serve, and if I do serve I will not be able to do it by myself. I have become more intimate with my wife, including having a couple of heated discussions with her, gratefully without alcohol, pills, or guns. I can see that the decision to run for alderman affects not just me but my whole family, and I am more available now to pay attention to the group conscience formed by me, my wife, and kids. And I can also listen to the group conscience consisting of the people who are gathering to support my candidacy.

I feel as if I have talked way too long, but I want to say one more thing. I have stayed out of politics before because I imagined that public service and corruption were synonymous. I am grateful to this program for giving me a way to see that I can be a trusted servant.

Thanks, Warren.

Hi. My name is Chris and I am a member of Al-Anon.

Hi, Chris.

Hi, everyone. I'm new to this meeting, although I have been coming to Al-Anon for many years now. I enjoyed your lead, Bea, and with respect to the importance of unity, I will borrow your framework as Warren did.

I'm sorry I was a little late, so I missed the introduction to the meeting. But since I arrived at the beginning of your lead about the First Tradition, I guess we are talking about Traditions today and I want to talk about the Third Tradition: "The relatives of alcoholics, when gathered together for mutual aid, may call themselves an Al-Anon Family Group, provided that, as a group, they have no other affiliation. The only requirement for membership is that there be a problem of alcoholism in a relative or friend."

My mom was obsessed with her weight, and every few weeks she had some different scheme that was designed to bring us all to the peak of health. She was mostly invested in controlling my dad's weight, and I never understood how he remained obese until he took me out to lunch a few times when I was already an adult. There was hardly a dinner at which the conversation didn't revolve around how our neighborhood was deteriorating because of whatever group of people moving in and driving property values down.

We must have moved half a dozen times in my childhood, always to get away from them, the ones who were ruining the neighborhood. On the other hand, both of my parents seemed totally indiscriminate in terms of bringing people from work, as long as they fit into their narrow band of acceptability. But acceptability included having some serious alcoholics and pedophiles staying at our house, including at least one who molested my younger sister.

What I have found in this program has been truly healing. The fact that I can come off the figurative street and become part of the meeting in this book is a gift of recovery. Anytime, anywhere there is a meeting where I belong according to the Third Tradition, I am a welcome member of the group. My race, religion, gender, and age are all irrelevant. All that matters is our shared common purpose. The only person who can tell me I don't belong here is me, and God knows I heard that message in my head often enough in the past.

The openness of this program helps me to carry the message of recovery. I have become interested in attending meetings in different formats recently. I have attended a number of online meetings, so when I heard that there would be a meeting in this book, I had a sense of my Higher Power calling me to participate. Thanks for giving me the opportunity.

Thanks, Chris, welcome to the meeting and keep coming back!

Hi. My name is Kelly, recovering alcoholic and member of Al-Anon.

Hi, Kelly.

Thanks for your lead, Bea. And welcome, Chris. Thanks for taking Tradition Three. I was about to jump in, but since I'm sort of new to this Al-Anon thing, I would have had to talk about the Third Tradition in AA. I am probably better off talking about Tradition Four: "Each group should be autonomous, except in matters affecting another group or Al-Anon or AA as a whole."

I am impressed by your willingness to join us at this meeting, Chris. I tend to become very attached to my routines. I go to the same couple of meetings every week: same time, same place, mostly the same people. I find routines comforting, and if I have to change the routine I feel anxious. Deviating from routines requires me to be assertive. So I go to the same meetings and people say to me "keep coming back, Kelly," as we did with you, Chris. So because I have been invited back, it's okay for me to continue coming to the meeting.

You see, when I was a kid my mother taught me that the height of rudeness was to show up somewhere uninvited, or almost worse was to invite myself. So I couldn't say to a classmate "Can I come over to your house?" because that would be inviting myself. So in case you're wondering how I got to this meeting, I'm here because my therapist told me to be here. And that's how I got to the couple of AA meetings I go to every week. I was in the hospital for the zillionth time, and someone finally had the idea that maybe I was depressed because I had a fifth of vodka in me most of the time. So they found these AA meetings for me, and I have been going ever since.

I get pretty disrupted when I have to go to a different meeting. Tradition Four is a pain in the ass for me. Because each meeting is autonomous, they are all just a little different. Sometimes the meetings last an hour, sometimes an hour and a half. Sometimes the meetings are speaker meetings where I get to listen and won't get called on to participate.

Other meetings involve discussion of topics, or the Steps or the Traditions, like this meeting. Some meetings you have to raise your hand to talk. Other meetings everyone seems to get a chance to talk. Sometimes we remain together as one whole group. Some meetings split into smaller groups. So much goddamn freedom that I can't predict what exactly will happen at the meeting. And then I don't know how I am expected to behave. I mean, what if I broke the rules and everyone just glared at me contemptuously?

I have been experimenting recently with some autonomous behavior that I had previously considered pretty repulsive. I won't go into detail here, because I don't want to embarrass Chris. So maybe I am getting some help in practicing Tradition Four in my own recovery. With that I'll pass.

Thanks, Kelly.

Hi! I'm Richard and I am a child of an alcoholic.

Hi, Richard.

I'll take a shot of the fifth. Tradition, that is. Sorry for the alcoholic humor, I just couldn't resist. "Each Al-Anon Family Group has but one purpose: to help families of alcoholics. We do this by practicing the Twelve Steps of AA ourselves, by encouraging and understanding our alcoholic relatives, and by welcoming and giving comfort to families of alcoholics."

It took a while for me to get it that this Tradition applies to me, that I am the family member who needs help. I used to think that I would come to meetings to become a better helper. I am gradually realizing that for me the whole program is about letting go of needing to help, change, fix, manage, or control anyone else. Simply by my speaking at this meeting I am carrying the message of recovery to at least one person who still suffers: me.

Our primary purpose here is so different from the primary task of my family of origin, where we were all dedicated to fixing my alcoholic mother. I have to say my alcoholic mother, because even to this day my siblings cannot speak openly about alcoholism. When I have heard others talk about walking on eggshells to protect the alcoholic, that rang so true for me. It seemed that we were struggling not to carry any messages, but to protect all of us from hearing the message that we were suffering. We had to understand that mother was the only one who was entitled to suffering, but that none of us could openly acknowledge what the suffering was about. Even when the suffering did not explicitly involve alcohol at all, but the death of my older sister when she was thirteen months old, we could not talk about our feelings. I remember only the ritualized trips to the cemetery every July 4 to commemorate the anniversary of her death.

Thanks for listening. I'll pass.

Thanks, Richard.

Hello. I'm Leslie, recovering Al-Anon.

Hi, Leslie!

Hi, everybody. I found myself figuring that it was my turn to talk about Tradition Six when Richard pleaded the fifth. Thanks, Richard, for including some humor. But then I wondered whether I was compliantly obeying some unspoken expectation that each of us would talk about a Tradition in turn. I also recognize that one of my character defects is setting up power struggles, so I will do my best to keep it simple. Tradition Six is: "Our Family Groups ought never endorse, finance, or lend our name to any outside enterprise, lest problems of money, property and prestige divert us from our primary spiritual aim. Although a separate entity, we should always cooperate with Alcoholics Anonymous."

Before I share about my past experience I'd like to express a couple of notes of gratitude for the Tradition. First I want to recognize that this Al-Anon meeting takes place in this book, but that this meeting is not the book. The book hosts this meeting the way a church or school would host a meeting. The second note of gratitude goes to Chris and the reader for joining us at this meeting, because without you all the rest of us have a special relationship with the author of the book. This special relationship is tantamount to an endorsement of the author and the book, so your presence here truly allows us to meet in accordance with this Tradition.

I have another more personal reason to be grateful for Chris's presence at the meeting. Like Chris's mom, my mother was also obsessed with diets, but in my mother's case, it was health food fanaticism. Food, at least the right kind of food, had a magical quality that would fix anything that disturbed us: The quest for the right diet, the best combination of foods, food that was grown under the correct conditions; one month we were forced to eat brewer's yeast three times a day, the next month it was raw liver and grapefruit juice for breakfast.

I also need to share that I am a recovering psychiatrist. And I am slowly coming to realize that I have done with therapy and recovery what my mother did with food. I have dabbled in countless personal growth adventures, therapies, and even a number of Twelve-Step programs, looking for some magical fix to repair my emptiness. Tradition Six helps me to see that I will not get help if I wander about endorsing, financing, or lending my name to all manner of outside enterprises, missions, and belief systems. My primary purpose is me, and I am grateful that we can be open in Al-Anon about this being a selfish program. And just as my mother kept all of us in the family at a distance with her food faddism, I know I can keep all of you at a distance with my attachment to every new mental health fad that comes along. For today I see that my selfish interest is best served by taking the help that you all offer me and sharing with you the benefit of my experience. With that, I pass.

Thanks, Leslie.

Hi. I'm still Warren, and still a recovering Al-Anon.

Hi, Warren.

I wanted to talk about the Seventh Tradition, but at the moment I realize I may be excluding the reader. I am not sure if the reader wanted to share about the Traditions.

The meeting is open for anyone to share.

Hi. I'm the reader.

Hi, reader.

I will listen for now.

Thanks, reader. Keep coming back!

Actually my uncertainty about whether I needed to make space for the reader to share relates to the Seventh Tradition: "Every group ought to be fully self-supporting, declining outside contributions." I see two important

parts of the Tradition, first that we are responsible for supporting our own work, and second that we abstain from receiving support from outside of this fellowship.

When I started coming to meetings, I noticed that at each meeting a basket would be passed around some time during the meeting, and most people would put a dollar in the basket. But sometimes a member would simply pass the basket, and sometimes a member would put in a couple of bucks. A member of the group, acting as treasurer, would collect the money, and the money would be spent on room rent, literature, or sent to the local or national service office. I was impressed that all of these financial transactions were voluntary, and I have never seen any status or prestige connected with a group member's financial contributions. In the same way that Leslie described the way in which we don't attach ourselves to outside enterprises, I see the Seventh Tradition as protecting us from outside enterprises attaching themselves to us if they are not really part of us and working with us. So I am grateful that we are all given the freedom in this program to participate and contribute in ways that are meaningful and appropriate to our individual needs.

This freedom has not always been available to me. I grew up with parents who had their separate bankrolls; Daddy held all of the economic power and Momma held the spiritual power. Daddy made it clear to all of us that we were not like so many other niggers, that he was a successful businessman, and he was staying with his family and supporting us. Since all of his business buddies were also his drinking buddies, his support of us was contingent on his attending his business meetings, from which he always returned drunk. His financial contribution to our family was not exactly voluntary; it was his cross to bear, what made him superior to the undependable, shiftless niggers. Momma, on the other hand, was proud of holding the family together because of her moral superiority; she had not let her husband abandon his family as so many of her girlfriends had. She was a veritable saint for putting up with his drinking and occasional womanizing. So Momma's morality also seemed not to be entirely voluntary, but more a result of martyrdom.

I am coming up now on an opportunity to make good use of this Tradition. As I prepare to run for alderman of my precinct, I would like to be an authentic voice for my constituents. The Seventh Tradition helps me be attentive to the risks I incur by accepting contributions from interest groups that do not necessarily represent or belong to the group of people who will be electing me. I cannot pretend that I can perfectly discriminate, so to speak, between contributors who are part of my constituency and those who are outside. I will need the continued spiritual guidance I receive from various friends and advisors, both in and outside of this program. With that, I pass.

Thanks, Warren.

This is probably a good time to mention the Seventh Tradition for this meeting. If this is your first meeting, this one is on us. Since the meeting is taking place in a book, we don't have a literal basket to pass around to collect money. We have no dues or fees, but if anyone present wishes to participate in the Seventh Tradition, you can send a dollar to your local service office or the World Service Organization for Al-Anon.

Thanks, Bea!

I'm Leslie, recovering Al-Anon.

Hi, Leslie!

I feel some shame about jumping in to share again so soon, but this is my favorite tradition, the Eighth Tradition: "Al-Anon Twelfth Step work should remain forever nonprofessional, but our service centers may employ special workers."

Some of my friends tease me about being a professional Al-Anon because I am a psychiatrist. I see it as part joke and part serious, since I do find myself often worrying about my patients and trying to get them to change rather than being honest with them about what is going on.

Tradition Eight gives me a boundary that I desperately need in my relationships with people. When I first heard in Al-Anon that I am not responsible for other people's feelings and behavior, I could not distinguish between not being responsible and being irresponsible. If I stopped prescribing Valium for my sick brother, he would become unbearably anxious, get drunk, and maybe then fly into a rage and hurt my parents. Once I used my professional status to medicate him, I convinced myself that to stop the medication was unprofessional. So I also couldn't tell the difference between being unprofessional and being nonprofessional. Just as I am not a professional in this group, I am not a professional in my family. I am my parent's child, my brother's sibling. This tradition also offers me a compassionate alternative to my own view of what it means to be a psychiatrist, which is tantamount to being God. The Eighth Tradition suggests a category of special workers, which I interpret to mean that each of us may occupy special roles that still do not require us to assume superhuman authority or responsibility.

I want to share one more story that I feel so much shame about that I can't believe I can tell it here. I suspect I may be responding to the pressure of this being my last opportunity to let go of this shame in this meeting and in this book. My father was admitted to the hospital where I was doing my internship. He had drunk himself into massive heart failure, ironically despite all of my mother's efforts to stave off heart disease with the right diet. Well, the right diet had also not prevented him from being seriously constipated, and his doctors were concerned that the pressure of attempting to move his bowels might aggravate his heart condition. But no amount of stool softeners seemed to help. Of course, no one told the doctors about my parents' fascination with colonic irrigation and all manner of laxatives.

I managed to discover all this by reading his chart, which I now understand was one of many boundaries I disregarded as part of my disease. When I went to visit my father the day before he died, he complained bitterly about the pain and cramping in his guts. I took it upon myself to stick my fingers in his ass to manually disimpact him. He died early the next morning and I have been convinced ever since that I murdered him. I never discussed any of my actions with his doctors, but when I asked indirectly what they understood the cause of his death to be, I could not accept or believe their answer: he had had such serious damage to his heart that he was unlikely to have lived more than a few days at the most. Even though I understand that self-blaming and over-responsibility are major parts of my disease, I continue to struggle with guilt. Thanks for giving me the opportunity to unload my secrets.

Thanks, Leslie.

Hi. I'm Richard, another "professional" Al-Anon.

Hi, Richard.

I'll talk about Tradition Nine: "Our groups, as such, ought never be organized; but we may create service boards or committees directly responsible to those they serve."

By the way, I will need to leave this meeting early, so if someone is talking when I get up, don't take it personally. I promised my wife that I would be home to take care of the kids. Besides, it's a great opportunity to demonstrate my understanding of the Ninth Tradition.

Building on Leslie's theme of the difference between irresponsible and not responsible, unprofessional and nonprofessional, I see in this tradition a distinction between disorganized and unorganized. The major obstacle to our being able to see Mom's alcoholism was the idea we grew up with that alcoholics were sloppy, staggering, incoherent messes. My mom's parents managed to remain in denial about Granny's alcoholism. Granny would be vivacious and chatty when she was moderately intoxicated. In her full-blown drunkenness she would become morose and almost catatonic. Grandpa, organized Prussian that he was, would revel in her wildness and then make excuses for her to friends and family as he trundled her off to bed when she became listless and despondent. By the time I was a teenager, Grandpa had her committed to the state mental hospital, where she was diagnosed as depressed and received regular shock treatments as well as dependable deliveries of gin from Grandpa. My mom had promised herself that her family would be different, and she kept her promise. Mom was always very serious, never flighty like Granny. We had set meal times and we went to mass punctually every Sunday. Mom drank only enough to keep a lid on her anxiety; fortunately for her thirst, she was an extremely anxious person. So she balanced her anxiety with her drinking much the way I understand some drug addicts balance their cocaine and heroin use.

Having grown up with all kinds of rules, spoken and unspoken, I have come to appreciate being able to embrace the chaos that enters my life, especially in my family now with four lively children. Being part of a meeting at which people can arrive late, like Chris, or leave early, as I will, without taking on the role of resented disrupter has been a refreshing change from the rigid structure my family used to protect itself from looking at its alcoholism. I also hope that my wife and I are able to serve each other and the family we have created in a responsible manner and not enabling each other to stay sick. Thanks for listening.

Thanks, Richard.

Hi. I'm Kelly.

Hi, Kelly.

Before you leave, Richard, I am going to give you a hug. I can't believe I did that. I guess I have become more attached than I let myself admit.

I should talk about Tradition Ten: "The Al-Anon Family Groups have no opinion on outside issues; hence our name ought never be drawn into public controversy."

As I was saying earlier in connection with Tradition Four, I become attached to routines and rules rather than people. That's why I was surprised by the spontaneous outburst of affection toward Richard. It's so unlike me, but I guess I haven't really known who I am through the haze of alcohol, pills, smoking, and now this family disease stuff. Between me and my mother, there were no inside issues. Everything revolved around what other people would think. That's why I am so grateful that this program does not have any rules. It's disruptive, I hate it, and I know it's what I need.

I am also reassured that each Twelve-Step program I go to focuses on one part of my disease. Sometimes I hear people complaining about having to go to two or three different meetings. For me it means that I can tackle one small piece of insanity at a time. I don't think I would have stayed in AA if they expected me to deal with my pills, smoking, or alcoholism in my family. And God knows the trouble I would get into if all of us drunks and addicts had to agree on any other outside issues such as politics, religion, or sex.

I am grateful that I have learned how to give and receive hugs here, even though I also know that hugs are an outside issue. We are free to hug or not hug, pray or not pray, share or not share. The freedom in program not to have opinions has also helped me to become a little less opinionated myself. With that I'll pass.

Thanks, Kelly.

Hi. Chris here. Still a member of Al-Anon.

Hi, Chris.

Thanks again, everyone. Tradition Eleven: "Our public relations policy is based on attraction rather than promotion; we need always maintain personal anonymity at the level of press, radio, films, and TV. We need guard with special care the anonymity of all AA members."

I want to add to Kelly's comments about Tradition Ten. I am grateful that for the purposes of this meeting, this book that we are meeting in is an outside issue, otherwise I could not be here with you right now. So I want to acknowledge how important the Traditions are for my recovery.

Back to the Eleventh Tradition. We have a public relations policy, which means we are mindful of the kind of relationship we have with others who are not part of our group. How different from my family of origin, as I was telling you earlier. We had no boundaries aside from bigotry. While we were busy keeping away those who we had determined were bad because of their race, religion, or ethnicity, we were entertaining all manner of self-destructive behaviors, such as drinking and overeating, as if we were advertising to the world: Please join us in killing ourselves because we are so full of hatred that we have no way to connect to one another by simply sharing our thoughts and feelings. That's what keeps me coming back, the fact that I can depend on having a place here where we can attract one another on the basis of shared experience rather than promoting something outside of ourselves.

I may be anticipating some comments about Tradition Twelve, but I want to share some of my initial confusion about anonymity. When I first learned about Twelve-Step programs and their beginnings in Alcoholics Anonymous, I thought anonymity was designed to protect those disreputable alcoholics from embarrassment about their awful behavior. So anonymity was all tied up with secrecy, and I imagined people going to Twelve-Step meetings with masks on their faces or hoods over their heads like at Ku Klux Klan meetings. When I got to meetings and saw people privately exchanging phone numbers, and even passing around a sign-up sheet to create phone lists for the meeting, I realized that my illusions of secrecy were not well founded.

I am impressed at the moment by how well anonymity is working in our meeting here. I am aware of having entered a meeting that takes place in a book, and yet I do not have a personal relationship with the author. It occurs to me that the author may be sitting here with me right now, that I really can't be sure that the person who is identified as the reader is not also the author. And all of you could not be sure that I am not the author.

Anonymity helps me remember that by myself in isolation I am not all that significant. I have to be willing to lose part of my previous individual identity to join with the world outside of me. And to the extent that I let go of various individual differences, including my race, ethnicity, and religion, I can become part of a larger enterprise, which doesn't mean hiding all of my individual attributes or being ashamed of them. If all of the rest of you have some connection to each other that I do not share, that would have made me an unwelcome outsider in the world I grew up in. Because we cherish anonymity, I belong here as much as anyone else.

To finish speaking about Tradition Eleven, I want to note that the author's anonymity in this meeting is being maintained at the level of press, and just in case this book is made into a movie, at the level of film as well.

Just as when I have been to Al-Anon meetings in churches whose ministers may also be in recovery, they show up in these meetings as regular people and not in their professional roles. I suppose I may as well share with you that, in my other life, I am a minister. Thanks again for welcoming me here.

Thanks, Chris!

My name is Bea, grateful member of Al-Anon.

Hi, Bea!

I guess I'm finishing this meeting by talking about Tradition Twelve: "Anonymity is the spiritual foundation of all our Traditions, ever reminding us to place principles above personalities."

Thank you, Chris, for introducing the topic of anonymity in your sharing about Tradition Eleven. I bet my therapist would confront me on getting into his head with this comment, but I think he would enjoy the idea that any of us could be mistaken for him by someone outside his professional world. Like Chris.

On a more personal note, thank you again, Chris, for helping me to understand and feel grateful for my therapist not being here at this meeting. I had been feeling hurt that he chose not to be here since this is the last chapter of the book. At the risk of idealizing my therapist, as my therapy group accuses me of doing, I can see his deep regard for the Twelfth Tradition in deciding not to attend this meeting. He would be violating his anonymity at the level of the press, and potentially compromising his recovery.

I can identify with the risks involved in sacrificing anonymity. As a writer myself, I decided some years ago to write a piece about my own recovery. I did not maintain my anonymity, and I lost my job soon thereafter. For a long time I blamed myself for the job loss and saw it as a just punishment for my crime of hubris. Only much later did I see that the loss of the job was inevitable. I needed to find different work that was more suitable to where I was in my recovery. The real harm I had done was to risk blaming my recovery for the job loss and then lose my recovery.

I further appreciate the trust that my therapist has in us to conduct an Al-Anon meeting with integrity, including the meeting's ability to embrace a member from outside the book, although I guess you understand, Chris, that you are in the book now. The integrity of our meeting has everything to do with our adherence, to the best of our ability, to the principles of recovery, and our letting go of the idiosyncrasies of our personalities.

We have come now to the end of our meeting. "In closing, I would like to say that the opinions expressed here were strictly those of the person who gave them. Take what you liked and leave the rest.

The things you heard were spoken in confidence and should be treated as confidential. Keep them within the walls of this room and the confines of your mind.

A few special words to those of you who haven't been with us long: Whatever your problems, there are those among us who have had them, too. If you try to keep an open mind, you will find help. You will come to realize that there is no situation too difficult to be bettered and no unhappiness is too great to be lessened.

We aren't perfect. The welcome we give you may not show the warmth we have in our hearts for you. After a while, you'll discover that though you may not like all of us, you'll love us in a very special way—the same way we already love you.

Talk to each other, reason things out with someone else, but let there be no gossip or criticism of one another. Instead, let the understanding, love, and peace of the program grow in you one day at a time.

Will all who care to join hands and recite our closing prayer. I put my hand in yours and together we can do what we could never do alone. No longer is there a sense of hopelessness. No longer must we each depend upon our own unsteady willpower. We are all together now reaching out our hands for a power and strength greater than our own. And, as we join hands we find love and understanding beyond our wildest dreams."*

Kelly, I would like you to have a newcomer packet. As chairperson for the meeting, I also need to let you know that in Al-Anon we do not introduce ourselves as members of any other groups, including other Twelve-Step programs, in order to respect the traditions.

Bea, will you ever stop putting me down?

Sorry if I offended you, Kelly. At Al-Anon meetings we offer to newcomers that somebody will be available after the meeting to answer any questions. So if you or the reader would like to talk to someone about anything that you did not understand at this meeting, feel free to contact Al-Anon Family Group Headquarters, Inc. by telephone at (757) 563-1600 or by e-mail at <wso@al-anon.org>. Would either of you like a hug?

---

*Al-Anon Closing, 1964, reprinted by permission of Al-Anon Family Group Headquarters, Inc.

Appendix A

Twelve Steps of Alcoholics Anonymous

1. We admitted we were powerless over alcohol—that our lives had become unmanageable.
2. Came to believe that a Power greater than ourselves could restore us to sanity.
3. Made a decision to turn our will and our lives over to the care of God *as we understood Him.*
4. Made a searching and fearless moral inventory of ourselves.
5. Admitted to God, to ourselves, and to another human being the exact nature of our wrongs.
6. Were entirely ready to have God remove all these defects of character.
7. Humbly asked Him to remove our shortcomings.
8. Made a list of all persons we had harmed, and became willing to make amends to them all.
9. Made direct amends to such people wherever possible, except when to do so would injure them or others.
10. Continued to take personal inventory and when we were wrong promptly admitted it.
11. Sought through prayer and meditation to improve our conscious contact with God *as we understood Him,* praying only for knowledge of His will for us and the power to carry that out.
12. Having had a spiritual awakening as the result of these Steps, we tried to carry this message to alcoholics, and to practice these principles in all our affairs.

Appendix B

Twelve Traditions
of Alcoholics Anonymous

1. Our common welfare should come first; personal recovery depends upon AA unity.
2. For our group purpose there is but one ultimate authority—a loving God as He may express Himself in our group conscience. Our leaders are but trusted servants; they do not govern.
3. The only requirement for AA membership is a desire to stop drinking.
4. Each group should be autonomous except in matters affecting other groups or AA as a whole.
5. Each group has but one primary purpose—to carry its message to the alcoholic who still suffers.
6. An AA group ought never endorse, finance, or lend the AA name to any related facility or outside enterprise, lest problems of money, property and prestige divert us from our primary purpose.
7. Every AA group ought to be fully self-supporting, declining outside contributions.
8. Alcoholics Anonymous should remain forever nonprofessional, but our service centers may employ special workers.
9. AA, as such, ought never be organized; but we may create service boards or committees directly responsible to those they serve.
10. Alcoholics Anonymous has no opinion on outside issues; hence the AA name ought never be drawn into public controversy.
11. Our public relations policy is based on attraction rather than promotion; we need always maintain personal anonymity at the level of press, radio, and films.
12. Anonymity is the spiritual foundation of all our traditions, ever reminding us to place principles before personalities.

Bibliography

Al-Anon Family Group Headquarters, Inc. (2000). *The Al-Anon Family Groups-Classic Edition.* Virginia Beach, VA: Author.

Alcoholics Anonymous World Services, Inc. (1953). *Twelve Steps and Twelve Traditions.* New York: Author.

Alcoholics Anonymous World Services, Inc. (1976). *Alcoholics Anonymous: The Story of How Many Thousands of Men and Women Have Recovered from Alcoholism,* Third Edition. New York: Author.

Bion, WR. (1961). *Experiences in Groups.* New York: Basic Books.

Brook, D. and Spitz, H. (Eds.) (2002). *The Group Therapy of Substance Abuse.* Binghamton, NY: The Haworth Press, Inc.

Brown, S. and Lewis, V. (1999). *The Alcoholic Family in Recovery: A Developmental Model.* New York: Guilford Publications.

Calamari, JE, Cox, WM, and Roth, JD. (1996). Group Treatments for Men with Alcohol Problems. In MP Andronico (Ed.), *Men in Groups* (pp. 305-321). Washington, DC: American Psychological Association.

Flores, P. (1997). *Group Psychotherapy with Addicted Populations.* Binghamton, NY: The Haworth Press, Inc.

Rice, AK. (1965). *Learning for Leadership.* London: Tavistock Publications.

Roth, JD. (1991). Application of the Tavistock Model to Group Psychotherapy for Recovering Addicts. In *Proceedings of the Tenth Scientific Meeting of the A.K. Rice Institute* (pp. 107-111). Jupiter, FL: A.K. Rice Institute.

Roth, JD. (2003). Alcoholics Anonymous As Medical Treatment for Alcoholism: A Group-Analytic Perspective on How It Works. In RM Lipgar and M Pines (Eds.), *Building on Bion: Branches* (pp. 145-163). London: Jessica Kingsley Publications.

Yalom, ID. (1995). *The Theory and Practice of Group Psychotherapy,* Fourth Edition. New York: Basic Books.

Index

Abstinence, 55-57
Addiction
    as family disease, 1-17, 41-44
        disruptions to group work, 3-4
        healthy group function versus
            diseased group function, 5-15
        models of human behavior, 2-3
        process of joining groups, 1-5
        telling one's story, 15-17
    letting go of, 116-117
    medication in treatment of, 87-91
    sharing nature of, 87-89
    unmanageability
        addictive personality, 41-44
        forms of intoxication, 39
        illusion as heart of, 40
        post-traumatic stress disorder,
            44-45
        resistance and, 40
Addictive personality, 41-44
Al-Anon Family Group Headquarters,
    154
Al-Anon program, 134
Alcoholic delusional jealousy, 40-41
Alcoholic personality, 41-44
Antabuse, 90
Attachment
    barriers to, 61-62
    maintaining, 111-112
    and sexuality, 91-95

Bion, Wilfred, 11
Boundaries
    crossing, 63-65
    regulation, 7-8, 9-11, 107-108

Defocusing, 57
Dependence, 11
"The Dream" (Pollak), 59

E-motion, 79
Experience in Groups (Bion), 11

Fight-flight, 11-12
Flores, Philip, 39
Free association, 33-36

Groups
    authority and, 47-58
        abstinence, 55-57
        agenda, 57
        assumption of power originating
            in, 47-49
        authorizing Higher Power, 49-50
        diagnosis, 52-53
        duration of treatment, 54-55
        hypotheses for authorization, 52
        substitution of therapy for
            addiction, 53-54
    basic assumption dependence, 11
    basic assumption fight-flight, 11-12
    boundary regulation, 7-8, 9-11,
        107-108
    carrying message of recovery
        conditions for being a group, 19-20
        criteria for, 21-25
        group mind, 25-26
        identification, 21-25
        limitation in thinking, 26
        spiritual awareness, 26-27
    disruptions to work, 3-4
    generativity and reproduction, 8-9